Praise for *It's*

Lauren does something beautiful in   he
shows the reader ways in which we s.   :ld
from the eyes of a five-year-old. From the beginning you feel encouraged
and inspired to look at life differently, and in a world where life can seem
crazy and chaotic a switch in viewpoints can be quite soothing to our souls.

—Jamie Ivey, host of *The Happy Hour* podcast

Lauren is a dear friend and mama who has journeyed through loss and
love. Her tenacity and tenderness bleed from these pages, and Mareto's
delightful life lessons will captivate your heart and keep you coming
back for more!

—Rebekah Lyons, author of *Freefall*
to Fly and *You Are Free*

Balancing personal history with mama-bear sensitivity, Lauren
Casper grabbed me by the hand and led me along a path of discover-
ing God's goodness through the lens of her child. There, in Mareto's
vibrant world of innocence and wonder, love is inexhaustible, community is essential, and generosity is a reflex. Life shimmers with hope
on the other side of *It's Okay About It*. I am grateful for their story.

—Shannan Martin, author of *Falling Free:*
*Rescued from the Life I Always Wante*d

This book is one giant mic drop. You're in the middle of a winsome
story and then, *Boom!,* Lauren brings it. Or maybe it's her son, Mareto.
Mostly—now that I think of it—it's Jesus. Which means, this book is
exactly what we all need. The simple reminders hold deep truths that
will help you recapture the joy of your one beautiful life. Don't miss this.

—Jennifer Dukes Lee, author of *The*
Happiness Dare and *Love Idol*

"Our children can be our greatest teachers if we let them"—one of the many sticky and spark-igniting truths in this new book from Lauren Casper. I read this book from cover to cover in only a few days, but that is because Lauren writes like the friend you entrust with your extra house key. I will be gleaning from this book for many years to come—remembering the rich, life-giving innocence Mareto offers me within these pages. Mareto now feels like my own. As I read, I watch him, hear him, and take him in as the tiny fingerprints of untainted love gripping my heart. Through his safe and simple language, we learn grand and important lessons in vulnerability, forgiveness, callings, and intimacy—undiluted and unfiltered. Mareto taught me how to love better, breathe deeper, and be "okay about it" more often. Each time I remember to position myself as a student of my own children, I will thank Mareto (and his mom, Lauren) for the gift of this great book.

—Kasey Van Norman, bestselling author

of *Named by God* and *Raw Faith*

We are all in the trenches—the trenches of loss, of acceptance, of turning over a new leaf, of caregiving, of keeping the faith. In *It's Okay About It*, Lauren Casper meets us in our trenches, bringing words of hope inspired by the honest language of her five-year-old son. Using his simple phrases, Lauren uncomplicates the complicated. Through the complexity of her story, we see the gentle bravery of motherhood and the transformative power of love.

—Mary Evelyn Smith, librarian and

blogger at WhatDoYouDoDear.com

Lauren Casper's vulnerable storytelling style makes for a delightful read! Her son and their journey is unique to them, but relatable to any reader who wonders where and how to look for God in unexpected places. I both cried and laughed out loud in public places while reading it, and found myself telling total strangers what had moved me.

—Beth Guckenberger, author, speaker and

co-executive director, Back2Back Ministries

You're going to *love* this book. Through Lauren's words and Mareto's wisdom, you're going to be drawn in to a delightful and encouraging glimpse of childlike faith. When you read, you'll be slowed down and captured by grace and goodness—and you're going to close the book each time you read feeling a little more peace and sanctuary right where you're at. Read it, pass it on to a friend, and read it again. You'll be nearer to the Lord and more at ease for it.

—Jess Connolly, coauthor of *Wild and Free*, author of *Dance Stand Run*

The Lord always speaks to us right where we are, but it's often in the trenches of messy, busy, weary motherhood that we forget he is right there with us—even speaking through the very children hugging our feet. *It's Okay About It* challenged me to slow down and hear how Jesus might be speaking to me through my children, to rest in the reminder that he is always there, and to follow him bravely no matter the depth of the water. Lauren's connections to Scriptural revelations through Mareto's words has spurred me to listen more deeply to God's voice in everyday moments with my loves too. If you find yourself called to deeper waters, this is a must-read to encourage you.

—Andrea Young, founder of Created for Care

Once I picked up this book, I couldn't stop reading! Lauren's writing is a gift of grace and tenderness. The stories of this beautiful family captivated me, and the profound and heartwarming lessons found in Lauren's book wrapped closely around my heart. Lauren tells her story in a powerful way that lets Jesus shine through the broken places, allowing us to see the light of his goodness. *It's Okay About It* will leave you hopeful, grateful, and encouraged.

—Courtney Westlake, author of *A Different Beautiful*

Brimming with joy, self-awareness, and truth, Lauren Casper's *It's Okay About It* is a must-read. This is a beautiful book, one that's written for all of us whose lives crave faith, simplicity, and wonder.

—Jessica N. Turner, bestselling author of *The Fringe Hours: Making Time for You*

We would all do well to stop and see our world a little differently. *It's Okay About It* helps me wipe the grime off my worldly lenses and see life with an innocent hope. Lauren's tender heart and tough mama-spirit make her son Mareto's story sing. This book is timely and needed for our sometimes cynical and hurting world.

—Hayley Morgan, coauthor of *Wild and Free*

You might not think that the key to shifting our often stubborn perspectives would be found by looking through the eyes of a five year old little boy. But Lauren Casper was given a beautiful gift in her son. Mareto's unique way of encountering the world is sure to challenge anyone's understanding of life, love and everything in between. In *It's Okay About It*, Lauren couples her wonderful storytelling with Mareto's powerful perspective to ignite a refreshing realignment we didn't even know our hearts needed. This book is a must-read that is sure to challenge your perspective, refuel your hope tank, and inspire you to live life wide open.

—Becky Thompson, author of *Hope Unfolding* and *Love Unending*, creator of Scissortail SILK and BeckyThompson.com

it's OKAY about IT

LESSONS FROM A REMARKABLE
FIVE-YEAR-OLD ABOUT LIVING LIFE WIDE OPEN

LAUREN CASPER

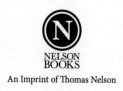

NELSON
BOOKS

An Imprint of Thomas Nelson

Published in Nashville, Tennessee, by Nelson Books, an imprint of Thomas Nelson.

The author is represented by Alive Literary Agency, 7680 Goddard Street, Suite 200, Colorado Springs, Colorado 80920, www.aliveliterary.com.

Thomas Nelson titles may be purchased in bulk for educational, business, fund-raising, or sales promotional use. For information, please e-mail SpecialMarkets@ThomasNelson.com.

Library of Congress Cataloging-in-Publication Data

Names: Casper, Lauren, author.
Title: It's okay about it : lessons from a remarkable five-year-old about
    living life wide open / Lauren Casper.
Description: Nashville : Thomas Nelson, 2017. | Includes bibliographical
    references.
Identifiers: LCCN 2016036957 | ISBN 9780718085421
Subjects: LCSH: Spirituality--Christianity. | Christian life.
Classification: LCC BV4501.3 .C4145 2017 | DDC 248.4--dc23 LC record
available at https://lccn.loc.gov/2016036957

Printed in the United States of America

17 18 19 20 21 LSC 6 5 4 3 2 1

For my little family—John, Mareto, and Arsema.
"We stick together."

CONTENTS

CONTENTS

Introduction

"It's Okay About It"

My son came into my life when I first dreamed of becoming a mommy. He was the wish and the hope I held in my heart for many years as I waited. Then one day a phone call came, followed by an email and a handful of attached pictures. The silent prayers now had a name and a face. Mareto. My beautiful, brown-eyed, brown-skinned boy with wide eyes and enormous hands and feet.

I came into Mareto's life on a warm and sunny January morning, in a redbrick courtyard in the bustling city of Addis Ababa, Ethiopia. My husband, John, and I walked through strong iron gates, crossed the brick courtyard, and knelt down in front of a tiny three-month-old boy in a green Bumbo seat. I carefully lifted him out, drew him to my chest, and we became mother and son.

Our path to Mareto was messy and hard, filled with

uncertainty, frustration, and tears, but the important thing was that it led us to him. In the moment when I first wrapped my arms around him, everything changed. It was the moment our dreams came true and we became a family . . . and it was beautiful. I knew that Mareto would change my life and make it better, but I had no idea just how much I would learn from him and with him as we worked through the challenges of this world together.

Now that we've brought him home, the journey is still bumpy at times. Real life is simply that way. We like to be in control, but so often things happen that are beyond our control. Every day can feel like a complicated board game without instructions. But Mareto, with eyes that twinkle and widen with curiosity and delight, reminds me that good exists and life is beautiful.

A few days after we met Mareto, we had the honor of sitting with his birth mom to answer her questions and ask our own. One particular question had been at the forefront of my mind, and when the moment was right, I asked her, "Does the name *Mareto* have any special meaning?" She simply smiled at me and said, "Peace."

I think about this often, the way God brought it all together with such purpose. I think about it especially whenever certain things pop out of Mareto's mouth.

Life with Mareto can be like playing the telephone game sometimes. He blurts out little phrases that have their origin in something he saw or heard, but by the time they make their way through his mind and back out of his mouth, they've transformed. At first they may sound silly, but when I stop to think about them, I see the amazing truths God is teaching me through my son's expressions. Sometimes life's most poignant lessons are learned in the least expected places, and sometimes the peace of God that overcomes our circumstances starts in the mouth of a child.

So when Mareto throws one of his phrases into an ordinary moment, I have learned to press pause and take a deeper look into my own heart to find extraordinary truth. For instance, when life feels overwhelming or confusing, it often shows up on my face; and because Mareto is such an intuitive little boy, he can immediately tell that I'm struggling. In those moments he sits next to me, pats my knee, or takes my face in his little hands and says, "It's okay about it." He doesn't usually know what "it" is for me, but he knows whatever it is . . . it's okay.

It's true. Maybe whatever I'm dealing with isn't okay in the moment, but eventually it will be okay—because we live in a world that can be a bit upside down, but we know love wins at the end of every day and God is still on the throne.

My grandmother passed away last fall, and Mareto found me crying at the foot of the stairway in our home. He sat beside me, put his hand on my back, and bent his face so that his nose was almost touching mine.

"You feel sad?" he asked me.

"Yes," I told him. "Mommy's grandma went to heaven, and that makes me feel sad because I miss her."

His sweet and genuine response to me was, "Aww. It's okay about it. You can go to heaven to see her."

He's right. He might not have understood fully what he was saying. Maybe he thought I could go visit her in heaven anytime I wanted. But the truth still remains: Though it didn't feel okay in the moment that my grandmother had died, it really was okay about it, because one day I will get to see her again. Within a few seconds and a couple of innocent sentences, Mareto comforted me with faith and hope and an eternal perspective.

So it is with many of Mareto's insights about life. A simple sentence or two will bring me back around to what is most important. His words point my gaze toward heaven and encourage me to live and love bigger and better than before.

God knows each of us intimately, and he knows how we tend to interpret our world. Mareto experiences the world in a unique way and shares it with those around him. I believe God knew when he determined that Mareto and I would go together just how much I needed a little boy whose name is *Peace* to remind me, "It's okay about it."

one

"Watch Out for Diesel 10!"

I know I'm biased, but Mareto is far too adorable for people not to notice. His head is covered in tight black curls that remind me of springs, and his cheeks are soft and squishy and always ready to smile. When we go out in public, strangers often try to talk to him.

We might be making our way down a grocery store aisle when it happens: A sweet older woman smiles and says, "Hello, young man!" Mareto looks up, pleased that someone is speaking to him, and blurts out, "Watch out for Diesel 10!"

I laugh as the stranger glances at me in confusion, and I awkwardly mention something about five-year-olds and Thomas the Tank Engine. She smiles, still confused, and walks away. Mareto has already retreated back into his own mind, but even so, he remains ready to warn the next person who might try to engage him in conversation.

This was Mareto's standard greeting for well over a year. We had different ways of explaining it to strangers, friends, and acquaintances. Sometimes we'd just keep walking. Other times we'd say how much he loves Thomas the Tank Engine movies, and occasionally we'd stop to explain that our son has autism and often struggles with the "right way" to engage with new people.

One day it hit me that in his own special way, Mareto was doing what most of us wish we could do. Many people—myself included—say that they're sick of shallow talk, and they would much rather get into things that matter when they talk to people. I think what they're really saying is that they want to talk about the things they care about, the things that make them . . . them. Yet they continue having the same surface-level conversations we all have every day, probably because it can feel rather awkward to actually dive into topics we're passionate about.

FEAR KEEPS US FROM FORMING RELATIONSHIPS.

It's scary to let people really see us right off the bat. We keep our barriers intact until we feel safe and have tested the waters to determine whether or not this is the crowd with whom we can be ourselves. Fear keeps us from forming relationships.

For me—and I imagine for most people—it's the fear of judgment that causes me to hold back and talk about things I don't really care about. It's just easier. After all, we're each unique, created with varying interests and gifts, so the things that make me excited might seem silly to others. But that doesn't mean we should hide those parts of ourselves.

For example, I love movies, and I always have. I love vintage Hollywood and current blockbusters. Give me Judy Garland and a bucket of popcorn, and I'll consider it a great day. Same goes for Sandra Bullock and a bag of Sour Patch Kids. Talking about movies, my favorite TV shows, and actors is fun for me because I'm interested in those things. But most of the time I wait to get to know people before I ever bring up the topic on my own.

Last summer I went out to dinner with a group of my girl-friends. These friends were fairly new to me because we'd moved to a new city and had only recently started attending their church. On the drive to the restaurant one of my new friends brought up an actress, and I lit up. Suddenly we were chatting about movies and actors with our heads close together. Our other friends laughed and mentioned how out of touch with that topic they were, but they also smiled as we talked because it was fun to see our enthusiasm.

Do you see my point? To every other person in that van, what my friend and I were discussing was shallow and meaningless. But to us it wasn't. We shared a similar interest, and we cared about our topic—silly as it was to other people. Soon we moved on from movies to donuts, and we began bonding over another shared love. Next thing we knew, we realized we had both grown up in California and had even more in common than we first realized.

Before, I had been afraid that perhaps my new friends would judge me as superficial or "worldly" if they knew how much I loved movies. A little voice in my head had whispered that it wouldn't look good for a pastor's wife to care about any of that. But that little voice was lying and talking to my insecurities.

My friend's simple comment about an actress she liked caused my guard to go down and opened the door for us to connect more quickly. I now consider her one of my dearest friends, and I love that I'm as comfortable chatting with her about movies as I am discussing more serious things, such as both our sons' developmental delays.

The path to connection with others can start with expressing joys we have in common, but it can also go the route of sharing heavier issues we feel deeply about. The funny thing is the way we sometimes avoid both types of conversation—which reflects the way we hide from each other.

Case in point: I may love movies, but I'm also passionate about bigger things, such as orphan care and prevention, global hunger and access to clean water, history and politics, race relations, education reform, and disability awareness and acceptance. But I tend not to lead off with those topics for fear of being viewed as "too intense." They are heavy, massive issues that I worry will make people uncomfortable, so I keep them to myself unless someone else leads the conversation in that direction.

One place where this changes completely, though, is the Created for Care Retreat. Every year, in February and March, I make the seven-hour drive from my home in Virginia to a lakeside resort in Georgia. Together with eleven of my dearest friends, we spend four days working as hard as we can putting on retreats designed to create an environment of rest, refreshment, education, and encouragement for nine hundred foster and adoptive mothers annually.

Women come to Georgia from all over the United States and Canada. Some missionary moms even fly in from the countries where they serve. Some are young mothers in waiting, and some are empty nesters who foster. Our educational, political, social, spiritual, and financial backgrounds are all over the map, but we all have one thing in common: our experience in foster care and adoption. Something truly special happens at these retreats. Invisible walls crumble to the ground, and strangers become sisters.

The first year I attended Created for Care, I came home and tried to explain it to my husband, John. It was my first time going away to something like this, and we both had worried that the money and time sacrificed wouldn't be worth it. But it was and then some. The word I kept returning to as I talked to John on the ride home from the airport was *relief*. I felt so much relief—relief and acceptance.

John looked confused by my description, so I tried to explain why I had such an overwhelming sense of relief. It was because I didn't have to hold back in my conversations. I was among friends, even though I'd never met the women at the retreat before. When we talked in the halls and corners and by the fire or over our meals, we didn't have to preface anything with a long explanation of "adoption-ese." We all already knew what a home study entailed, why the wait was so hard, what "cocooning" meant, and what a trauma anniversary was.

Having a shared language and experiences, we could skip over the first eight steps of new friendship and had the freedom to simply talk about the things we cared about and what mattered to us. The result was instant connection and acceptance. Not having to put forth extra effort either to explain myself or to hold back and keep things to myself could only be described in that one word: *relief.* I hadn't realized how hard it had actually been to not go there with the people in my life. I didn't realize how tired it had made me to constantly hold back in relationships.

Christ's example in Scripture shows us a relationship model that is very different, though. When I read through the New Testament, I see story after story of Jesus wasting no time to connect with people's hearts. The beautiful thing is, not only does he get straight to their hearts, but also he does it differently with each person—knowing that we are unique. What opens up the woman at the well is different from what opens up his relationship with Zacchaeus.

As I watch each story play out, I see Jesus drawing people out with simple questions or statements. There was no deep theology or fancy explanation—just an acknowledgment of who they were, or a question about who they wanted to be. The result was an individual coming to life.

When Jesus met the Samaritan woman at the well, he

asked her for a drink. It might seem insignificant to us, but that question opened up her world. She knew it was unusual for Jews to speak with Samaritans, and her interest was immediately piqued. When she asked him about it, he responded, "If you knew the gift of God, and who it is that is saying to you, 'Give me a drink,' you would have asked him, and he would have given you living water" (John 4:10). Just like that, Jesus went from zero to sixty, from asking for a drink of water to sharing the gospel with a woman he had met only moments ago. It wasn't coincidence; he knew which words would open her heart to him.

The story didn't stop there, of course. He went on to ask her about her husband, which again prompted her to share more of her story. In turn, Jesus told her all about her life and the good news. She left marveling at this exchange and wondering if he was the Christ—all because Jesus saw her and asked for a drink of water.

As Jesus was passing through Jericho on another day, he stopped at the base of a tree. A short man named Zacchaeus was perched in the branches, hoping to get a glimpse of Jesus. Jesus looked up into the tree and told Zacchaeus to come down because he was eating at his home tonight. Instead of a glimpse, Zacchaeus got dinner with the Christ! As the townspeople muttered about Jesus dining with a sinner (Zacchaeus was a tax collector), Zacchaeus repented and Jesus proclaimed, "Today salvation has come to this house, since he also is a son of Abraham. For the Son of Man came to seek and to save the lost" (Luke 19:9–10).

Zacchaeus developed a relationship with Jesus because of a request to dine together. Can you imagine if Jesus had stood at the base of the tree and the two had exchanged greetings before awkwardly conversing about trees and the view and the weather? There would have been no relationship.

Thankfully, Jesus is the ultimate example of getting to the heart of the matter and skipping over things that don't. His purpose is clear, and it is, I believe, also what we all crave: relationship. We were made to connect to one another, and we crave meaningful relationships; but we let our insecurities build a wall between us and others.

It's scary to put ourselves out there, to ask questions or invite others to our homes and into our lives. It's hard to take the time to share what makes us tick, why we live the way we do, or how our past has changed us. It's scary to share who we are, because we can only hope the world loves us and accepts us.

But it's beautiful when we swallow our fear and open ourselves up to finding friends who don't judge, with whom we can share understanding and love.

This is part of what makes the Created for Care Retreats so special. You can tell another mom that you let your child eat a snack thirty minutes before dinner, and she won't judge you. Instead, she will assume your child has known starvation, and a snack is a way to reassure that little heart that in your home there will always be enough food. You can bring up the fact that you haven't gotten a sitter in eight months, and instead of assuming you put your children above your marriage, other moms will understand that your child likely has extreme separation anxiety or connecting issues. They can understand how you are going through a season of building foundations that weren't established at the beginning of your child's little life.

It's also beautiful to discover a friend who loves the same television show, music, or sport as you do. That person who lights up whenever you talk about football together becomes a safe place, and you progress from discussing college brackets to problems at school or struggles with finding the right church. In the same way, because I found common ground talking movies with my friend, it led to conversations about our shared home state, cultural differences, and later, even race issues in our country. Isn't it incredible how it all starts with a simple connection and then moves into a deeper relationship?

When Mareto greets people with his loud, "Watch out for Diesel 10!" he is sharing what makes him light up! He reminds me of my own desire to connect with others around the things that make me tick. Maybe Mareto is actually the one who knows the "right way" to introduce himself to others. Mareto doesn't have the barriers that urge me to test the waters first, so nothing holds him back from letting people into his world right away.

I want to live like that.

two

"Christmas Is Ruined!"

I sat on the couch, holding my breath, watching Mareto play with a pile of squishy rubber blocks. It was a warm summer morning, and Mareto was quiet and focused as he placed one block on top of another. I was silent, afraid to move and ruin his process. A little stream of drool began running from the corner of his mouth, a sign that he was really working hard to concentrate.

He reached over to the pile and grabbed another block to place on top of the first two. When he carefully set down that third block to form a small tower, I burst into cheers of joy and excitement as he looked up at me with pride in his eyes. I clapped enthusiastically while tears streamed down my face.

My husband and I had spent three mornings a week for almost a year sitting in a room covered with mats and

10

watching the occupational therapist play with our son. As they played, she explained all the steps that our brains take to do something as basic as stacking three blocks.

On this day, Mareto was finally taking those steps.

What we once would have considered effortless and unimpressive was actually the result of hard work, many mistakes, and a great amount of energy. I thought about how much we take for granted, and I realized what a gift it is to feel this level of joy over my child stacking blocks. Then I laughed out loud when Mareto began working on a new tower—this one five blocks high.

Sometimes life can be an absolute mess for a while before things start to come together the way we had hoped. When it doesn't go the way we expected, we have to shift our mind-set to create a new definition of success. Mareto may desperately want a large rectangular block to sit steadily on top of the tiny square block, but no matter how many times he tries, the block will keep toppling over and the tower just won't rise.

Life is exactly like that. Sometimes we have to step back, re-examine, and try again . . . this time reaching for a new block. Maybe it's not the block we originally wanted to use, and we need to apply a different vision to the project. Maybe things are taking longer than we expected, don't look as pretty as we had hoped, or are more difficult than we antici- pated. Life doesn't always look the way we want it to.

When this happens, Mareto shows his frustration by loudly lamenting, "Christmas is ruined!" I don't know where he got this phrase, and while it is an overly dramatic way to express disappointment, it's also strangely familiar. More times than I care to admit, I've looked at failures in one season of life and felt that my entire story was ruined.

Becoming Mareto's mommy looked nothing like I thought it would. I spent years desperately trying to make a large rectangular block balance steadily on my tiny square block. Everyone else had large rectangles, and I tried to build a tower that looked like theirs.

Month after month became a "try again" month as John and I hoped for a baby. Month after month, then year after year, my failure to conceive was spotlighted by other people's successes. As friends announced pregnancies, I cried in the bathroom. Christmas cards joined their torn envelopes in the trash can, because the smiling faces of happy new parents told a story that reminded me of all I was missing. My Christmases felt ruined.

Friends innocently made jokes about not drinking the water at church because a baby boom seemed to be happening. As if it were that easy. I listened to women talk about their family plans and how many children they wanted, spaced perfectly apart by three years. They didn't know what a luxury it was to believe they held that kind of control over their lives.

It was supposed to be simple, right? It was easy for everyone else, so what was wrong with me?

When the doctors finally told us that it wasn't possible for us to have children, I was completely devastated. My heart was broken as my dreams of motherhood fell and shattered at my feet. I silently lashed out at God, at friends, and at myself. I felt like an utter failure.

Thankfully we have a gentle, patient, and gracious God who led me out of my grief. He began to show me that he had never intended for my tower to be built with rectangles. Instead, he had given me a completely different pile of blocks.

When John and I started the adoption journey, it looked a bit like Mareto stacking his blocks: pure concentration and determination. It wasn't always pretty. Many nights we stayed up late poring over paperwork. The timing never worked out the way I hoped, and the waiting was excruciating.

Sometimes when I looked to the left and the right and saw my friends making plans, I wished my journey looked like theirs. Their rounded bellies held their babies safe and secure as they talked about nurseries and names. I cried into my pillow in the dark, hoping our child wasn't hurting or hungry. I breathlessly counted down to court dates as my friends talked about routes to the hospital and birth plans. Everything seemed so effortless for them.

I held on to the assumption that once their babies were born and once Mareto came home we would all be on level playing fields again. We would all be parents caring for babies, and my tower would finally look like everyone else's.

I was wrong.

At first I thought that the trials during Mareto's initial months home were common to the adoption experience. Then I began to notice that not only were we not on the same path as my friends with biological children, but my friends who had adopted children were living a completely different experience from us.

I felt alone, frustrated, and baffled by the differences in our family. Why couldn't Mareto sit through church with me like all the other babies? When the congregation sang or applauded, why did he cover his ears and cry hysterically? Why did Mareto panic when we tried to get a babysitter to watch him? All the other kids were learning words. Why didn't my son call me "Mama" too? Mothers shared milestones on Facebook, and I cried behind my computer screen.

Then, when Mareto was about eighteen months old, he stopped progressing entirely. He had been sleeping through the night for about six months, but suddenly he wouldn't sleep at all. Night after night we took turns rocking him, but he would scream for hours until finally collapsing around six a.m. He refused all food except plain oatmeal, and the few words he had learned around age one disappeared as he stopped talking altogether.

Mareto's doctor ran all kinds of tests. I was convinced he had caught some rare bug, and if we could just find it and treat it, the issues would be resolved. I didn't know much about autism, so I had no idea that Mareto was exhibiting several classic signs of regressive autism.

Our quest for answers eventually led us to a speech evaluation, where, after two hours of testing, we learned that Mareto's speech was delayed (which we already knew) and that he would need speech therapy a couple of times a week.

Then we were informed that Mareto also showed several red flags for ASD, so they recommended he be evaluated for that as well.

Neither one of us had heard the term *ASD* before, so I asked what it meant.

"Oh!" said one of the therapists. "Autism spectrum disorder."

The air left my lungs, and I whirled my head around to see John's reaction. Red patches were rising on his neck and face. He was holding back tears. I was too.

We walked out of the room with our son just moments later and made our way to the car. We sat there in silence and shock. This wasn't what we'd expected, wasn't how we'd planned to build our tower. How would this fit into the narrative I had prewritten for us of a meaningful, successful life?

I'm learning that life is often like that. What we see as setbacks or standstills are actually turning points in our story. We see failure, but God sees progress and gently nudges us to keep walking, or crawling, forward—to pick ourselves up and try again and again and again.

We tend to define success in quantitative terms. We want to be able to measure it in order to feel that we have accomplished something. It could be easy to

WHAT WE SEE AS SETBACKS OR STANDSTILLS ARE ACTUALLY TURNING POINTS IN OUR STORY.

look at Mareto finally stacking his blocks as the moment of success, but what about the months of hard work that preceded that moment? Just because we can't see results doesn't mean we aren't building a successful life one moment, one effort, one step at a time.

I'm learning that God often works that way in our lives—quietly behind the curtain, moving all the parts to create something beautiful and unexpected. But because I don't have his perspective, and I can't see the plan for building my unique life, I complain and worry. Because I can't see ahead to the end, I look to the left and the right and see everyone else's seemingly perfect lives. That's when I begin to feel that our story is falling apart . . . that our Christmas is ruined.

For years I watched families send out announcements, plan baby showers, and set up nurseries. And I thought our life's story was less valuable, less beautiful, and less successful. Sometimes I look around and see friends building houses and buying new cars and sending their children to fancy schools, and I think we're falling behind. I get on my computer to see children reaching milestones, and I glance down at the big brown hands still playing with blocks—and wonder if what we are doing matters . . . if our story is important too.

Expectations can set us up for disappointment and unrealistic ideas of what our journey should look like. If we aren't careful, we focus too much on a vision of the American Dream that says anyone who works hard enough can have their version of a perfect life. But the truth is, someone can work as hard as possible at something and never achieve it. There is heartbreak and brokenness hiding behind all that hard work.

Maybe your spouse left or died young, and you find yourself single and wondering how to move forward—how to build a life again. Maybe you're a stay-at-home mom wondering if you should have taken a different life path. Maybe you wonder if your friends with careers have more successful lives. Maybe your life doesn't look like what you dreamed of when you were seven or ten or eighteen years old.

Our paths in life can be frustrating and confusing, but we keep going no matter how messy things look. Our journey might be unpredictable, but we are building the tower and finding our way one block at a time.

So how do we redefine success? We start by taking an eraser to our expectations. My friend Beth says, "Expectations are premeditated resentments."

I'm a planner by nature. I plan our vacations and schedules, and I even map out my trips to the grocery store. I'm more comfortable with a plan. So when life throws me for a loop, I get frustrated, resentful, and angry—or scared stiff—because I've set myself up for that reaction. It can be tempting to see failure instead of a different version of success.

I'm especially guilty of holding unrealistic expectations during the holiday season. Holidays are stressful for most people, and it all goes back to expectations. We place them on ourselves, and others place them on us too. We all want Christmas to look like a Hallmark card.

Sweet children in rumpled pajamas open gifts on the floor by the tree while the adults sip coffee by the fire, smiling at the sounds of ripping paper and delighted squeals. In the kitchen voices softly chat about family over chopped vegetables and simmering gravy. A football game plays in the living room while dads assemble toys. Then the culmination of the day: the Norman Rockwell image of a family sitting down to a feast. Joy and peace and love.

But Christmas usually looks a bit different from that. Mareto spent his first few years completely confused and overwhelmed by the holiday. He didn't understand what to do with the packages placed in his lap, and he kept trying to creep out of the living room to lie down with the dog. There were no quiet afternoon hours of baking and football, and there were more tears than squeals of laughter.

A couple of years ago on Christmas Day, Mareto finally just lost it. After trying to process the hype of the day, he gave up and gave in to an epic meltdown. John disappeared with Mareto for hours as he tried to calm our son, and finally, they wound up in bed under Mareto's weighted blanket with the iPad.

I crept upstairs as dinner was being put on the table and found them both in bed—sweating a little and looking weary. John gave me a tired smile in response when I whispered, "How's he doing?" A few minutes later we all made our way downstairs. Mareto lay with the dog while we all ate and enjoyed our dinner with only a few interruptions.

At the end of the day, after several more episodes of

crisis management, we went to bed as we do most days—exhausted but happy. There was one big difference between this Christmas and the previous years: We went in with open hands and no expectations. We redefined success and found that Christmas, in fact, wasn't ruined. It was just our own version of success.

Glennon Doyle Melton, of the popular blog *Momastery*, encourages her readers to throw out the idea of *carpe diem* (seize the day) and instead choose *carpe kairos* (seize the moment).[1] Since when did success mean a perfect day? What if we looked for the good moments in hard days and deemed that successful?

A life that is full of sharp left turns, mistakes, loss, and taking chances is beautiful in its own way. When we walk through different seasons of life, we don't always recognize the foundations we're building. We don't see that we are placing that first or second block on the table and that it might be six months, six years, or never that we see the third block of the tower. We forget that our story is a crucial piece of a bigger story.

I open my now-worn, leather-bound pages to Hebrews 11 and find relief:

> By faith Abel offered . . .
> By faith Enoch was taken . . .
> By faith Noah constructed . . .
> By faith Abraham obeyed . . .
> By faith Sarah received . . .

By faith Isaac and Jacob blessed . . .

By faith Moses left . . .

And all these, though commended through their faith, did not receive what was promised, since God had provided something better for us, that apart from us they should not be made perfect. (Hebrews 11:39–40)

When I think about these men and women held up as heroes in the Christian faith, I realize just how imperfect they and their stories were. Their lives often looked messy and unsuccessful. They may have come to the end of the day—to the end of all their days—and looked back, wondering if they had lived a successful life. And if they could have wondered, it only makes sense that we would as well.

We know the end of their stories. We know just how much they mattered, and that's why we can have the courage to keep trying, keep fighting, and keep following our path. We, too, have faith that our story matters.

Recently John had a Monday off work. We were excited to drop the kids off at school and then enjoy an hour or two of peaceful conversation at a local coffee shop. But as we pulled into Mareto's school, the empty parking lot told us his school was closed that day—a fact I had somehow forgotten. Just like that, our plans for a "perfect" morning flew out the window.

As we drove our daughter to her very open school, I wondered what on earth we would do. John thought we could go to the coffee shop anyway and take Mareto with us, so that's what we did . . . for four minutes.

We ordered our coffee and pastries, got Mareto a cookie, and handed him the iPad. Within minutes of sitting down, his eyes began darting around the restaurant as he rocked in his seat. Seconds later he was crawling under the table, and from those signs of anxiety and overstimulation, we knew it was time to grab our cups and to-go bags.

As we drove to the playground to finish our breakfast while Mareto played, John turned to me and said, without a hint of sarcasm, "That went really well!"

I couldn't stop my laughter.

It was true. We were thrilled with how well Mareto had done. He had lasted four whole minutes at the table. We viewed the morning as a huge success, because we knew how far he'd come.

A successful life is measured in successful days, and successful days are measured in successful moments. Successful moments hide in places where we don't think to look at first, but they are waiting there to be celebrated.

Christmas isn't ruined after all. It just looks a little different this year.

three

"You're Making Me Feelings"

School can be hard for Mareto. I pick him up every day at three p.m., and some days the conversation during the car ride home goes like this:

"Did you have a good day, buddy?" I'll ask.

"Yes," Mareto says distractedly, as he looks at the toys left in his seat that morning at drop off.

I try again. "What did you do at school?"

"Nothing." This time his response is a little frustrated.

"Who did you play with today?" Maybe this question will bring up a fun memory.

"Mommy, can you give me some privacy? You're making me feelings." Mareto's voice is wobbly, and he's on the verge of tears.

Now I know it wasn't a good day, and he's feeling sad and frustrated and maybe even a little angry about it. I want him to let me in, but he wants privacy and I respect his need for me to stop questioning. We get home and snuggle on the couch—he wants me close by and longs for comfort, but he doesn't want to talk about it.

Mareto feels things on a grand scale. It goes beyond what is typical for most children his age, and because his feelings overwhelm him, he's had to learn how to respond to them. At moments I will kneel in front of him to see the emotions playing out across his face, and I feel as though I'm looking into one of those magnifying mirrors in the makeup section of the department store. I feel all those same emotions; I've just gotten really good at hiding or downplaying them.

Our culture tends to recoil from tears and negative emotions. I remember an older woman sharing a story with me years ago. She had been married for a long time before her husband passed away, and she missed him terribly. Every year on their wedding anniversary, she had dinner at home and sat alone thinking about the man with whom she had shared a life. It was a sad tradition, but one she needed. She loved thinking about the life and family they had built together through the years, even though the memories caused her pain because of how much she missed her husband.

One year a well-meaning friend invited her out to dinner on the night of her anniversary. My friend explained why she couldn't go out that evening and was met with opposition: "Oh, don't sit at home feeling sad! Come be with friends and have fun." My friend wisely refused, but she was met with further confusion and even judgment from the woman who simply wanted to protect her from grief.

We've gotten ourselves a bit confused, I think. We're tempted to view negative emotions as the enemy, and in doing so we ignore our emotions altogether instead of responding to them in a healthy manner. Instead of accepting that we will at times feel sad or angry, we pretend we never feel that way and cover it up with a night out or an extra bowl of ice cream.

A couple of years ago at Christmas, Mareto got a Buzz Lightyear action figure from his aunt and uncle. Of all the toys he opened that Christmas, he was the most excited about Buzz. With the push of a button Buzz's wings would pop open from his back, and off Mareto would go—running through the house making flying sounds. Another less exciting feature of the Buzz toy was that his wings would pop off entirely from time to time, and it took a bit of strength to get them back on. Mareto found this extremely frustrating.

One day we watched from the kitchen as Buzz's wings popped off yet again. Mareto let out a growl and, through gritted teeth, yelled, "I get *mad* sometimes!" as he threw Buzz to the ground. Our reaction was mixed: We were thrilled that Mareto had voiced his feelings but not so thrilled that he threw his toy. So I added an item to my list of things to work on with Mareto: responding well to emotions.

That week I wheeled out the chalkboard (also a Christmas gift) and drew four faces. One was happy, one was excited, one was angry, and one was sad. I wrote the corresponding emotion above each face and had Mareto point them all out. Then we talked about a time when he felt each emotion (excitement at Christmas, happy at the park, sad when Daddy went to work, angry when Buzz's wings popped off). For as long as he was engaged in the conversation, we talked about how to react to each feeling.

I got to sadness and explained that it's okay to be sad. When I asked him what he does when he feels sad, Mareto answered, "I really cry." I told him that crying is good, that it's okay to sit and cry, and that I would love to comfort him whenever he felt sad. I went on to tell him that a good thing to do when he feels sad is to come get me so I can hold him until he feels better.

Sometimes I don't follow my own advice very well. I catch myself saying, "It's okay, don't cry!" and I remember that I have told Mareto it's okay to cry. When I feel sadness and tears welling up in my heart and eyes, I take deep breaths and try to swallow them away. I don't want to cry and feel sad, but stuffing my emotions under a fake smile has never worked well for me.

I was twenty-three years old when I had my second miscarriage. It came just ten months after the first, and I wasn't ready for it. You are never ready to lose a child. I had just gotten off a roller coaster of emotions and was still worn thin from grieving our first loss. I didn't want to go through it all over again. I was scared.

It was a gorgeous July morning, and I sat on my bed looking out at the puffy clouds against a blue sky. The day didn't match my feelings, and I tried to pray through my tears. I remember the void, the raw pain of my heart. I remember feeling the weight of grief, and instead of letting myself give in to the tears filling my eyes, I turned off the valve to my emotions.

I started going through the motions of life as if nothing had happened. When pregnancy announcements or baby shower invitations came in the mail, I refused to cry. I also never smiled over them but simply threw them in the trash. I built a wall of stone around my heart to protect myself from pain, but it also kept out the love and joy and grace that God wanted to shower over me. I was miserable and numb.

Instead of accepting comfort by reaching out, I bottled up everything inside and let anger, bitterness, and resentment grow. Of course, I didn't know that my behavior and denial were self-destructive. I really believed I was protecting my heart.

Then John and I learned that I couldn't carry a child. By my twenty-fourth birthday, everything I thought I ever wanted was broken. There was a crack in the wall I had built, and new pain made its way inside. Soon the walls came crumbling down. I was tired of faking it and tired of pretending life didn't hurt. And in my exhaustion I quit fighting against my grief.

Once the people I loved saw how much I was hurting, they surrounded me with friendship and comfort. I let myself cry and feel sad, because something I loved had been taken from me. The loss of my two unborn babies and the dream of carrying a child inside of me were sad, and there was no fixing it.

Once I let myself cry and feel grief, I was able to accept—not get over—our losses, then get up and carry on.

Sometimes Mareto asks me to sing him the "sad song." When he was a couple years old, we downloaded a *Daniel Tiger's Neighborhood* app to our iPad because he loved the show so much. One of the games is about emotions, and each one gets its own song. The song about sadness tells children that it's okay to cry and be sad, but also it encourages them that eventually the sad feelings will leave and they'll feel better again.

Mareto loves that song in particular, and I do too.

In a simple little chorus we find acceptance, validation, and hope. Feeling sad is normal; no one can go through life only feeling joy or excitement. But hope and twinges of joy can exist amid our grief when we believe that someday we won't hurt as much.

Scripture points to the importance and value of all our emotions as a response to life. There's an entire book of the Bible titled Lamentations. A lamentation is defined as weeping, or a passionate expression of grief or sorrow—not your polite sniffle into a tissue. To lament something is to outwardly express the full agony felt in your heart, because there are moments in life when no other response is appropriate.

Ecclesiastes 3:4 tells us there is "a time to weep, and a time to laugh; a time to mourn, and a time to dance." This tells me that weeping and mourning are just as important as laughing and dancing. To watch Mareto laugh and dance is to come alive—because when Mareto laughs, he laughs so hard he gives himself the hiccups. It's hilarious and refreshing to see a little boy experience joy with his whole body.

Once we figure out that our emotions aren't something to avoid or hide away from the world, we find freedom. We open the door to relationships, because others will see our sorrow and join us, or find our joy contagious. Emotions are an invitation to let others in.

I love the Pixar movie *Inside Out*, and I have to confess that I cried several times throughout the film. It's the story of what goes on inside the head of a little girl named Riley.

EMOTIONS ARE AN INVITATION TO LET OTHERS IN.

The movie starts with newborn Riley's first memory—the moment she opens her eyes and sees two loving parents smiling over her. We, the viewers, are then zoomed into her mind, where the main character, Joy, emerges from darkness.

Joy is Riley's first and primary emotion for most of her childhood years. She does, of course, have other emotions, and they make up the rest of the cast. When Riley is still a toddler, Joy introduces us to the other four main emotions in the "headquarters" of Riley's mind.

"That's Fear. He's really good at keeping Riley safe.

"This is Disgust. She basically keeps Riley from being poisoned. Physically and socially.

"That's Anger. He cares very deeply about things being fair.

"And you've met Sadness. She . . . well, she . . . I'm not actually sure what she does."

Joy can find a positive purpose for absolutely every emotion, except sadness. She cannot figure out why Riley would ever need to or should feel sad, so she spends a lot of time trying to keep Sadness away from Riley's memories and the command center. She just can't figure her out.

But after a move from Minnesota to San Francisco turns Riley's world upside-down, Sadness wants to touch—and according to Joy, ruin—many of Riley's memories. Things begin to fall apart, and Joy and Sadness become unlikely companions in a mission to rescue Riley.

Toward the end of the story Joy and Sadness are separated. Joy pulls out a memory of Riley after a hockey game, and she remembers Sadness telling her how terrible Riley felt in that moment because she had missed what would have been the winning shot of the game. Then Joy watches the memory continue and sees Riley's parents and teammates surrounding and comforting her, and Joy has an epiphany.

"Sadness . . . Mom and Dad . . . the team. They came to help . . . because of Sadness."

Sharing our emotions, including sadness, brings people together. Sadness serves a vital purpose for our health and well-being because it's an honest reaction to the disappointing, hard, hurtful, and tragic things we experience. To present any other emotion is a lie.

Last week was Christmas, and we spent the week at my parents' house. Mareto loves going to visit his Grandma, Pap, and their dog, Toby. When the day came for us to return home, Mareto was so disappointed that our amazing vacation had come to an end. The corners of his mouth drooped, and his voice became quiet as he said good-bye to his grandparents.

As the car turned out of the neighborhood and my waving parents disappeared from view, big tears poured down Mareto's cheeks. Through his tears he wailed, "That makes me sad!"

I turned around to comfort him but stopped myself just before uttering the words, "Don't cry. It's okay."

Why shouldn't he cry? He just had a wonderful week with his grandparents, whom he used to see nearly every week when we lived only fifteen minutes away. Now it's a four-hour drive, and we don't get to see them as often. That's sad, and hard.

I reached my hand back to hold his, told him it was okay to cry, and said I was so sorry he felt sad. He cried for a little while, told me several times that he just wanted to go back to Grandma and Pap's house, and eventually he felt better.

But what if he had faked it? What if he had pretended everything was fine when he was crying on the inside? I would have assumed he was okay, and Mareto wouldn't have received the comfort he needed to feel better. Now Mareto knows he can tell me when he's sad. He knows that crying is a good and appropriate reaction to hard things.

Temple Grandin, one of the world's most incredible autism advocates, explains why having healthy and appropriate responses to our emotions is so important:

Boys who cry can work for Google. Boys who trash computers cannot. I once was at a science conference, and

I saw a NASA scientist who had just found out that his project was canceled—a project he'd worked on for years. He was maybe sixty-five years old, and you know what? He was crying. And I thought, *Good for him.* That's why he was able to reach retirement age working in a job he loved.[1]

It's not wrong to be sad, but for some reason we act as though it is. Perhaps if we own and value our own emotions, it will create a domino effect and others will feel safe being open with theirs as well.

Since Mareto is so open and pure with his emotions, I've realized the importance of owning mine. He's taught me that it really is okay to be sad or lonely or angry. Sometimes we just need to lean into our feelings and, in doing so, share a piece of ourselves with those we love.

four

"The Hill Is Very Tired"

It was early summer, and I had an itch to go hiking. My husband is always ready to spend the day in the woods, and he couldn't pack the bags and load us all into the car fast enough. There's a state park about forty-five minutes from our home, so while John drove I looked over the various trails on the park map. My goal was to find a short trail that wouldn't be too tough for the kids, and I found one that looked promising.

We entered the state park and began searching for the trailhead, but it was quickly evident that the map I held in my hands didn't match the actual layout of the park. So we ditched our plan and drove until we found a sign that promised a short hike of just a few miles. We unloaded the kids and our backpacks and started walking.

After about five minutes, we came upon a young couple on their way back. They warned us that the hike was pretty steep in places and was about three and a half miles total. They looked at our children as they mentioned these facts, surely thinking that we were slightly crazy for bringing two preschoolers on a hike.

But we pressed on, telling ourselves that we could turn around anytime we wanted to. The kids were having a blast getting dirty, collecting rocks and sticks, and inspecting bugs. The climb got steeper, and we kept going—until suddenly, Mareto halted at my side and let out a sigh.

"What's up, buddy?" I asked.

"The hill is very tired," was his weary response.

I followed his gaze to see that he was staring at the trail ahead and the mountain looming in front of us. I asked if he needed a break, but he just shook his head, grabbed a stick, and kept walking. So we all followed suit.

And we just kept walking, stopping occasionally for short breaks. Mareto sometimes tripped and fell, but he always got back up and kept moving. He never begged to go home, and he never gave up. A few times he reached out for our hands, and once he asked for a piggyback ride. But it wasn't long before he was ready to hike on his own again, to grab patches of moss or to stop and look at a spiderweb.

It was a beautiful and rewarding day. We were all exhausted on the ride home and devoured our dinner that evening. Later that night, after the kids were tucked into bed, John and I marveled at the strength our children had exhibited. We had no idea they were capable of hiking three and a half miles, half of which went up a fairly steep hill.

They'd surprised us, and it reminded me how we sometimes surprise ourselves too.

Mareto had just celebrated his first birthday when we decided to start the adoption process for our second child. It was a simple decision that looked nothing like the months of consideration, prayer, and discussion leading up to our first adoption. One night, I finished rocking Mareto to sleep and laid him in his crib before joining John on the couch. I gave him a sideways glance and said, "I want another baby. I want to adopt again." Then I held my breath and waited.

"Me too. Let's do it!"

It was that easy. The next day we sat down to discuss agencies and emailed our social worker. That was September 2011. We worked as tirelessly for our second child as we had for Mareto. We stayed up late filling out paperwork and completing parenting education classes. I brainstormed new ways to raise funds for each upcoming payment, and as we wondered about who our next little one would be, our hearts grew with love for a still unknown child.

In March 2012, though, amid the throes of this second adoption process, we started noticing significant changes in Mareto. The more obvious signs of autism were beginning to pop up, but we didn't yet recognize them for what they were. We pressed forward with the adoption as we lined up appointments and tests for our son, maintaining a generally positive attitude throughout the spring and summer. We thought we'd find Mareto the help he needed, and things would go back to "normal."

On Friday, June 9, I logged onto Facebook after laying Mareto down for his afternoon nap. I mindlessly scrolled through my newsfeed when a status from a fellow adoptive mother caught my eye.

"We have a new baby girl, twenty days old, in Ethiopia, with missing digits and webbed digits, who is in great need of a family right away. If anyone knows of families who have a completed home study and might be interested, please direct them our way."

Something stirred inside of me. My heart began to pound, and I found myself emailing for more information. I texted John, who was at lunch with a friend, and told him to come home as soon as possible. I tried to slow my emotions, knowing that John might not feel the same way about this baby girl whose name we didn't know and whose face we hadn't yet seen. But I couldn't slow down. My heart just knew. She was meant to be ours.

By the time John came home, I had already received her file from the adoption agency working to place her. We looked through her information and then scrolled through the twenty-plus pictures on my computer. I looked at John with pleading in my eyes; I would have jumped on a plane that evening if left to my own devices. But, ever the voice of reason, John suggested we take the weekend to discuss, think, and pray. So that's what we did.

By the end of Sunday it was abundantly clear that this stunning, tiny, three-week-old baby girl named Arsema was our daughter. So Monday morning we officially accepted her referral and gathered our paperwork for the Ethiopian government. We gave Mareto her picture and told him that the baby was his new sister and that she would be home soon. He couldn't speak yet, but his enormous smile told us he understood.

A month later we received a court date of July 30 and booked our flights to Ethiopia. In the midst of all the flurry, we continued securing appointments for Mareto. I spoke with a speech therapy office, who could get us in the day before our plane was to take off—so we took the slot and began packing our suitcases.

The day we walked into Mareto's speech evaluation, we were completely unaware of what the future held. After about two hours, we walked out with the words *autism spectrum disorder* still ringing in our ears. On the car ride home I tried to make sense of what it might mean for our family if Mareto did in fact have autism. As I overanalyzed every moment of the evaluation, John placed a calming hand on my knee and told me to slow down. We would take this day by day . . . but today we needed to finish packing.

By the next afternoon we were on our way to Ethiopia. When I began to worry about Mareto, John once again reminded me that we were going to take life day by day. And that day, we were going to focus on the little girl we were about to meet. So I set my concerns and fear aside and began to think about Arsema. It made for a beautiful week of falling more deeply in love with our new daughter.

When our plane landed back in the States, my heart was

full of concern for the daughter I had been forced to leave in Ethiopia while we waited for visa approval from the US Embassy. But since there was nothing we could do about that, our day-to-day once again turned to finding out what was going on inside of Mareto.

We had a new appointment lined up for September 5, and on that day our wonderful little Mareto was officially diagnosed with autism. Three weeks later he celebrated his second birthday, and two days after that, I boarded another plane bound for Ethiopia. It was time to bring our little girl home.

The three weeks between Mareto's diagnosis and bringing Arsema home from Ethiopia were filled with a lot of self-doubt. When we'd first learned about a little girl waiting for a family in a country on the other side of the world, we had no idea that Mareto was three months away from being diagnosed with a lifelong condition that would drastically change our daily life. Would we have made the same choice if we knew? Today the what-if seems unbearable. What if I had known what the future held and therefore held back? We wouldn't have a beautiful, spunky, incredible little girl brightening our lives every single day. No, that alternate ending is too painful to consider for long.

The truth is, at the beginning of this climb, I didn't think I could do it. I was tired and worried that the journey was too difficult and steep, and that I wasn't strong enough to make it. Amid the three weeks between learning Mareto had autism and bringing Arsema home, I cried on my sister's living room floor. I told her and my mom that I was so afraid I couldn't parent well. I didn't want to let down Mareto or Arsema, and I wasn't sure I would be enough for them. The future seemed so hard, and I was tired just thinking about it.

It was a painfully honest moment for me—one I think most of us have had at some point in life.

Maybe it's the weight of a ministry that wasn't supposed to be so hard. Maybe your church family, whom you love and have dedicated your days to serving, has turned on you and hurt your family. As you walk through the doors of that church each Sunday, maybe you think to yourself, *This is too hard. I don't know if I can do this. I'm tired.*

Perhaps you've just entered your second trimester and your husband left for a twelve-month deployment. It's your first baby, and you always thought you'd get to experience those first days, weeks, and months together. Now you're trying to figure out who can drive you to the hospital or help you in the middle of the night when you're exhausted and afraid. So you sit on the couch in a puddle of tears, missing your husband and thinking, *I'm so tired, and this is so hard. Can I do it?*

Or maybe you are like my beautiful, brave friend Sarah. She gave birth to an adorable little boy named Micah a couple months before Mareto came home. The boys spent their first two years of life as best buddies before we moved away. We started our second adoption process around the same time Sarah announced she was pregnant with their second baby. That July she would learn the sex of the baby at her twenty-week ultrasound, and I secretly hoped it would be a girl so Arsema would have a special friend just like Mareto had Micah.

The day of Sarah's appointment came, and we learned she was expecting a little girl to be named Evie. We also learned Evie wouldn't be with us for long, as she had several conditions incompatible with life outside the womb. All of us who love Sarah and her family were devastated. Over the next sixteen weeks, before Evie was born, I spent many moments on Sarah's couch talking about the fear, exhaustion, and dread she felt. It seemed completely unbearable to carry a child and deliver her into the world only to say good-bye.

But day by day, Sarah woke up and lived life. Then one night Evie came and graced us with her precious presence for four incredible hours before going home to heaven. It was excruciating. Sarah has to live the rest of her days without her daughter, and it hurts. It's hard and some days utterly exhausting, but Sarah is doing it.

We can do more than we think we can.

Life surprises us, and the future looms ahead of us like a giant mountain. It seems insurmountable, and we don't think we have the strength to climb it. We get tired and discouraged.

But we can all take a lesson from Mareto on that trail last summer. We can sigh, express our feelings about the situation, and then take another step. Day by day we keep walking. We will fall down sometimes. Some days will be messy, and we'll go to bed feeling bruised and beaten up by life. Other days we'll need help. Just as Mareto took our hands for support when he was tired or stumbling, we can reach out to the people who can steady us.

But, most importantly, we need to reach out to our Father, our one true Source of help.

I've found that when I am at my most discouraged and frightened it is because I've forgotten where my power comes from. It's then that I remember a simple verse I memorized long ago: "I can do all things through him who strengthens me" (Philippians 4:13).

Whatever God has called us to do, he is able to empower us to do it. We have access to his strength and power if we would just reach out and ask for it.

WHATEVER GOD HAS CALLED US TO DO, HE IS ABLE TO EMPOWER US TO DO IT.

Maybe I'm not strong enough to parent eight children or work a seventy-hour-a-week job, but that's okay because God hasn't asked that of me. He has asked me to be Mareto and Arsema's mom. And that morning on my sister's living room floor, with our future as a special-needs family looming in front of me, it all seemed more than I had the ability to handle.

Then I got up off the floor and took the first step. I took another step and another. And the day-by-day journey turned into months and years, and today I look back and see what a sweet life God is making for us, all because we trusted him.

I see that what I once feared has become my greatest treasure, and I can't imagine life without the two children I hold today. Arsema is Mareto's best friend and greatest cheerleader. She's brought joy and light into every single day. Mareto blossomed when his sister came home, and learning about how he experiences the world has only made us all better people.

Sometimes God takes us on an exhausting, uphill path. We stumble and fall and think we can't do it, but when we get up and take our Father's hand, we find that together we can do more than we ever thought possible.

five

"My Batteries Is All Gone!"

We were at a party one Sunday afternoon following church. About fifty people were gathered in the living room of our friend's home. The house was filled with the smell of potluck food, the sounds of laughter and loud conversation—each person trying to be heard above the noise—and the movement of adults chasing small children from room to room. It was overwhelming to introverted adults like my husband and me, but to Mareto it was nearly unbearable.

He started looking for his escape in the kitchen, and when he found a freestanding cupboard, he tried to climb inside. But there wasn't enough room, so he settled for standing inside and closing the doors as far as he was able. We looked over to find his little shoes peeking out from under the partially opened doors. Before we could get to him, our friend walked up and asked him not to stand in the cupboard. He initially obeyed but tried to get inside again several times.

Eventually we got Mareto settled on the floor with a large puzzle, then we turned back to the conversation we were having with friends. A few minutes later I turned to check on him, but Mareto wasn't there! I did a quick scan of the room and didn't see him, and that's when the panic started to build. I stood quickly and caught John's eye as we both started moving through the house looking in corners— any nook or cranny where Mareto could be hiding.

A minute later (that felt more like an hour) I saw John kneeling by a window in the front of the house. There, by his knees, I saw two little shoes standing between the window and the drapes. I rushed over and knelt down as well. Mareto was muttering something, and John was smiling at me. As I leaned my ear closer to Mareto's mouth, I heard it: "XTY394...JXW478...VXC211..."

I looked out the window to see what he was seeing: rows of cars lined up outside the house. And then I saw the license plates. Mareto was reading them, car by car, until he reached the end of the row. Then he'd start back at the beginning. Letters and numbers. Stability.

Mareto had reached his limit at this party. There was too much noise, too many smells, and too much activity. His sensory system was maxed out, but Mareto did what we so often do not do: He recognized that it was all too much, and he found a way to get the break he so desperately needed. He knew his limit, and he also knew how to find relief.

Letters and numbers never change; they are stable and constant. When hiding in the cupboard didn't work for Mareto, he found another way to escape—a window, drapery, and license plates. By focusing on something soothing, he was able to drown out his surroundings.

You see, back then Mareto had very little verbal ability. He couldn't tell us what he wanted to eat or what his sister's name was, but he knew his letters and numbers. He couldn't tell us he needed a break, so he just found a way himself.

These days Mareto has the words, and when it gets to be too much for him, he cries out, "My batteries is all gone!"

I love that about him.

The other night I sat on the couch with John as we looked over our plans for the month. I have a large dry-erase calendar that hangs near the kitchen for us to keep track of our activities and obligations. A few days prior, at the beginning of the new month, I'd taken great joy in erasing the previous month's scribbles to make way for a fresh four and a half weeks. I had numbered the days of the month and written down the three or four events I knew about. Stepping back, I'd sighed and relished that fairly clean slate. But it wouldn't last long.

We had our normal routine—work and school, plus my regular Bible study—and there had not been too much extra . . . until John brought home his monthly calendar and the kids brought home their school folders.

So that night on the couch we sat together and went over "all the things," as my friend Jessi calls them. At one point I put my head in my hands and said, "I feel like my brain is going to explode!" And I wasn't kidding. I felt pressure and panic and an overwhelming desire to quit everything.

Why? Because I was doing too many things, overloading my system, and running on fumes. And so was John.

It wasn't good for us—not for our marriage, not for our kids, not for our ministries, and not for our jobs. We can't give the best of ourselves to anything when we're living in a constant state of burnout. I don't want to do "all the things" okay-ish; I want to do a few things *well*.

It looks different for everyone, but my few things are faith, marriage, motherhood, relationships, and writing. Yet with a bunch of other items on the calendar and on the list weighing me down, I can't give my best to any of the core parts of who I am.

> I DON'T WANT TO DO "ALL THE THINGS" OKAY-ISH; I WANT TO DO A FEW THINGS *WELL*.

There's a lot of pressure today to say yes. Things move at a faster pace than ever before, and we have to keep up with so much. We have jobs, relationships, social media, church activities, school activities, sports, ministry, and more. And if we don't recognize—or if we just ignore—the signs of overload, we will soon find ourselves on the couch thinking our heads will explode. We need to know when enough is enough and when to say, "You know what? My batteries is all gone. I'm saying no."

The week before we traveled to Ethiopia to bring Mareto home, I was approached by a man at church who wanted to use our home for a weekly men's Bible study. I was surprised by the request since this person knew we were about to bring our first child home, and that Mareto was sick and would need a lot of extra care and attention. But the people pleaser in me absolutely hated to say no. I felt so much pressure because my husband was on staff at the church and we lived in the parsonage. So I did what any good wife would do . . . I passed it off to my husband!

John asked me how I felt, and when I told him it felt like too much, he responded with, "Well, that's that! We'll just say no." After we said no, the group found a new location for meetings, but I felt incredibly guilty for the next couple of weeks . . . until Mareto came home.

There was absolutely no way we could have hosted that study, and God knew it. Rocking my son each night, administering medications, soothing him every two hours, and getting used to a brand-new lifestyle was more than enough for me in that season. But when things are ministry-related they can be even harder to turn down than other types of requests. That's when I have to remind myself that it's not wrong to need a break, and it's okay to retreat from ministry and other self-imposed responsibilities for a while.

I love the story of Jesus feeding the thousands of people

after teaching them for hours. Stories like this inspire me to service, and when I read in Mark 6:34 that "he saw a great crowd, and he had compassion on them, because they were like sheep without a shepherd," I want to do more for my fellow man. But I also simply cannot ignore what Jesus did after teaching and feeding the crowds.

He retreated.

Verses 45–46 tell us, "Immediately he made his disciples get into the boat and go before him to the other side, to Bethsaida, while he dismissed the crowd. And after he had taken leave of them, he went up on the mountain to pray."

Yes, even Jesus needed a break. Why? Because in his time on earth he was fully man, and man needs rest. We need rest from our work, our ministry, and even our relationships. Jesus could have gotten into the boat with the disciples; in fact, it would have made more sense to us (and to them) if he had. After all, a storm was brewing, and Jesus knew his friends would be scared—so he probably should've gotten in the boat to comfort them, right?

Wrong.

There will always be more work to do. There will always be ministry waiting and people in need. Matthew 26:11 says, "For you always have the poor with you, but you will not always have me."

Jesus said this to the disciples after they expressed their shock over a young woman "wasting" an entire jar of perfume by pouring it over Jesus and weeping at his feet. They thought she could have done better by selling the jar and giving the money to the poor, but Jesus pointed out that there will always be people in need. Spending time with him was the better choice.

Our culture can tend to be works-driven. Even the various denominations that claim grace above all else (and really mean it) still find themselves driven by quantitative results and tangible evidences of faith. I grew up in the Lutheran church, and our favorite verse to claim as the cornerstone of our faith was Ephesians 2:8: "For by grace you have been saved through faith. And this is not your own doing; it is the gift of God."

We, rightly so, rejected the idea that works could get us into heaven, but did we live like we believed it? I'm grown now and the wife of a pastor, and I see why the number of pastors quitting due to burnout is steadily growing.[1] If we really believe that life isn't about works, then why are we killing ourselves constantly trying to do more? If we really believe that our faith is about a relationship and not our deeds, then why do we spend more time creating committees and planning events than we do following Christ's example of praying alone on a mountaintop?

There's nothing wrong with committees and events. Service projects are great, and Bible studies create growth in both spirit and relationships. But when these things are happening at the expense of our pastors' and our own well-being, then it's time to scale back.

It's not just true for church; it's true for all of life.

Yes, there is goodness behind so much of what we do

and participate in during the course of the week. The PTA helps us raise money for our schools and plan fun activities for our students. The basketball team helps teach our children coordination and how to work with others. Gymnastics instills a sense of pride and accomplishment in our kids, and the annual Christmas concert allows us to beam with pride over our preschoolers.

Facebook keeps us in touch with friends from childhood that we would otherwise lose contact with and helps keep extended family in the loop. Instagram helps us document our lives and keep everyday moments forever in picture form. Twitter is a wonderful tool for activism, and Pinterest provides inspiration and entertaining projects for many families. Though we like to point our fingers at social media as the root of our problems, there is nothing inherently wrong with it.

In the end, it's not necessarily *what* we're doing that is the issue; it's *how* we're doing it. Life is swirling around us, and we feel pressure to keep up. But we don't do very well at scaling back, taking on a reasonable amount of responsibility, and stepping away to rest every now and then. I ignore the twitch under my eye that essentially serves as a flashing red light, shouting, "Warning! Warning!"

Then things in my life start to break down one by one. I snap at my husband and criticize the way he does the smallest thing. Or I blame him for not helping more or working too much. I get short with my kids for not being perfect little angels every second of the day. I resent the email asking if

49

I'll bring some baked goods to the Christmas reception, and I feel dread when friends ask if I can go out for an evening.

I stare at my inbox with an overwhelming desire to just hit Delete on every single item while I mindlessly scroll Facebook. I stare at a blinking cursor on a blank screen and wonder where I'll find the words or the inspiration or the energy. I check out from reality with Netflix and cause further backup in my schedule.

My sleep is restless, and my temper is short.

I don't know what Mareto's inward warning signs were that day at the party when we found him reciting license plates. His outward sign in those days was trying to find a hiding place. Today the signs remain similar. Mareto will try to hide, rock himself in a corner, or blow an incredibly short fuse.

But the amazing thing about Mareto is that he's in tune with the warnings within himself—perhaps more so than the rest of us generally are—and he finds a way to get the rest he needs. Thinking back to that party, I'm so impressed with his resolve. He tried several times to retreat to the cupboard but was intercepted by an adult each time he tried to climb inside. But instead of giving up, he refused to be deterred by the interference of others and found his escape.

Now, back to John and me on the couch.

After I exclaimed that my head was going to explode, John got up to brew me a cup of tea, and I sat in silence for a few minutes. Then he came back, tea in hand, and we pulled the calendar up on his phone. Just three weeks until Christmas break—we could do this. But when I started factoring in travel plans to see family, the friends we promised to make time for, and the house projects we'd been putting off, I knew it wasn't going to be much of a break at all.

So we did something we wouldn't typically do: We said, "Enough." We scheduled extra vacation days and blocked off the calendar to give our family the break we so desperately needed. Then I skipped Bible study that week and snuggled on the couch with Arsema while we watched a Disney movie in our pajamas. I actually scheduled in some quiet, alone time in my personal calendar—something I had never done. And in the end, it was the best thing for all of us.

I want to give my best to the people I love and the work I'm called to; I'm sure that's what we all want when it comes down to it. But we can only do that if we recognize the signs of overload in our lives and know when to say, like Mareto, "My batteries is all gone."

SIX

"HERE'S SOME GOLD DUST!"

On any given Saturday morning, I can walk through the living room to find Mareto and Arsema excitedly crying out, "Gold dust!" and tossing imaginary fistfuls of it into the air. I love to watch them giggle and grin and delight in their little game. At some point Arsema will open her hands and say, "Oh no! Mine is all gone!" Mareto then says in his sweet, upbeat voice, "Here's some gold dust!" and pours some from his hands into hers. Then the game continues as they toss the gold dust into the air and dance around.

I'm always touched by Mareto's innocent and generous expression of love. Somewhere along the way he figured out what so many of us have forgotten: It is better to give than to receive. Why? Because love, and the giving of love, doesn't divide; it multiplies.

When Mareto pours his imaginary gold dust into

Arsema's hands, the game doesn't end. It continues with enthusiasm. It doesn't occur to Mareto that giving away his magical dust will mean less for him. It only means that he and Arsema can continue having fun together.

It's a tough world that we live in. Racial tensions, a refugee crisis, mass shootings, terrorism, recessions, and more. When things get hard or scary we tend to lock the doors and circle the wagons. We think that if we can just keep the shades drawn and the outside world on the outside, somehow we will have created a safe place.

On June 17, 2015, nine lives were taken in a senseless, racially motivated shooting at the Mother Emmanuel Church in Charleston, South Carolina. My friend Jessi Connolly lives less than three miles away from the church and received many messages throughout the night inquiring about her family's well-being. The next morning Jessi posted a response on Facebook, and a particular piece of it resonated in my heart:

> Friends have checked in to see if we're safe, and I'm not sure how to answer. Physically, we're safe, and we're held by Jesus. But I don't want to feel safe in a city where my neighbors don't feel safe.

I don't want to feel safe in a city where my neighbors don't feel safe.

Another way to say that would be, "I don't want to hoard safety in a city where my neighbors don't have the same safety."

Why is our natural inclination to build walls rather than to tear them down? I read somewhere that new babies, when startled, jerk outward. Their reflex response to fear is to throw their arms and legs out in a reaching manner. Over time, though, they learn to self-protect, so older children will respond to a loud noise or an object flying their way by flinching inward—hunching their shoulders, ducking their heads, and wrapping their arms around themselves.

Life has a way of teaching us that it's every man for himself. So we become hoarders—of safety, privilege, money, material items, and even love. We fear giving them away, because we don't really believe it will result in an increase of those things. We see it as a loss for ourselves.

In the wake of the refugee crisis, the terror attacks in Paris and California and Florida, and beautiful little boys washing up on the shores of Turkey, there has been a strong reaction from those of us here in America. Some have cried out for us to refuse entrance to immigrants and refugees, while others have cried out for us to welcome them with open arms.

One response is fear-based, like the older child flinching at a loud pop. During his presidential campaign, when asked for his stance on immigration, Donald Trump repeatedly said he will build a wall along the Mexico–US border and make Mexico pay for it. Late-night shows drew a lot of jokes from this statement, but amid our laughter and eye rolls, we can miss the real tragedy of the statement: when we build walls, we're always the ones who pay for it.

What and who are we missing out on when we put up walls, lock our doors, and circle our wagons?

I received an email a couple years ago from a young man who had come across my blog. He wasn't trying to be rude but asked a question that felt rather harsh and hurtful. He wanted to know "what would possess" (his words, not mine) us to adopt not one, but two children of a different race and of varying degrees of special needs.

Because ... love.

It was a Tuesday night in October when my plane touched down in Norfolk, Virginia. With Arsema strapped to my chest in the Ergobaby carrier, I walked off the ramp, through the gate, and into the arms of John and Mareto. Just like that, we were together for the first time as a new family of four.

WHEN WE BUILD WALLS, WE'RE ALWAYS THE ONES WHO PAY FOR IT.

A little over an hour later, we walked through the front door of our home, and after a warm bath and a bottle, we laid Arsema in the bassinet next to our bed for her first night of sleep at home with us. We gently closed the bedroom door and turned around to find Mareto standing in the hall, staring at the closed door. We tried to nudge him into the living room, but he wouldn't budge.

We walked down the hall but turned when we heard his sniffs and muffled cries. What we saw was a foreshadowing of the remarkable relationship Mareto and Arsema would go on to create. Mareto sat on the floor of the hallway, his face pressed into our bedroom door, and softly cried, "My baby" through his tears.

Any worries I had about the impact a new baby would have on Mareto vanished in that moment. He loved her and hated to be separated from her even for a night of sleep. For weeks and months I thought maybe it was a fluke, that soon he would grow fed up with this new person who invaded his space and changed our routine. But it never happened.

Today people love to comment over the special bond they share. Other parents marvel over how much they love each other, and I do too. But I believe it started that first night when Mareto cried for his sister on the floor of the hall, and it continues as they consistently choose love and generosity toward each other.

Moms expecting their second child tend to worry about how a new baby will impact the status quo of the family. They also wonder if they'll be able to love a second child as much as their first. I know this because as we waited to bring Arsema home, so many moms would share these secret fears with me and then follow it up by saying, "Don't worry if you feel this way. It's normal." Then they would reassure me that they loved their subsequent children every bit as much as their first.

Why? Because love doesn't divide or diminish as it's given away.

Bringing Arsema into our home multiplied the love and joy of our family a hundredfold. Mareto blossomed when he became a brother. Having a daughter has brought out such a tender side of John, and I love sharing my lipstick with a little girl with an infectious laugh and lashes for days. We gave our hearts and lives away once more to another person, and in return our family, our hearts, and our capacity for love grew.

Somewhere along the way we forget that we all belong to each other, and when we give of ourselves—our time, money, our possessions, and our love—we all gain.

I love the way Jesus explains it in Luke 6:38: "Give, and it will be given to you. Good measure, pressed down, shaken together, running over, will be put into your lap. For with the measure you use it will be measured back to you."

Give and it will be given to you. Give and everybody gains: the giver and the receiver. Not just a little, but pressed down—like brown sugar packed into a measuring cup to fit in every ounce of sugar possible. Shaken together, to get just the right amount ... and running over, overflowing with love and joy and hope. Two now hold what one once held, and neither forfeits their half of the original measure of grace. Each now holds a whole measure.

Love doubled. And those who are the recipients of love are more likely to turn around and give love away themselves. So love will then quadruple, and so on. Do you see how rapidly love multiplies when we give it away?

Years ago, when we were working hard to bring Mareto into our family, we held a large yard sale to raise funds for his adoption. Friends from church donated items they no longer wanted, and soon half our church parking lot was filled with tables full of secondhand items. A handful of girls from the youth group set up a little bake sale at the end of the parking lot, and I had high hopes for the day.

I had read blogs and Facebook updates from friends who had done similar fund-raisers and was excited by the final dollar amount they were able to raise. I expected similar results, but when we counted up the money at the end of a very hot and exhausting July day to find that we hadn't even come close to meeting the goal I had in mind, I was incredibly disappointed.

There were enough items left over to hold another yard sale, so we decided to try again the next Saturday. That week I did some serious soul-searching. We hadn't lost any money on the yard sale; in fact, we had raised a modest amount of funds. Dozens of people had donated items, and friends had helped out in the blistering heat. So why did I feel so disappointed?

I continued to dwell on why I felt empty, tired, and frustrated by the results of our first yard sale. Then, about midweek, it dawned on me: I had been acting incredibly selfish. After reading all the blogs by other adopting moms about their incredible yard sales, I had presumed that we would receive the same amount. I was so focused on getting rather than giving that what we actually *did* receive didn't matter . . . it hadn't been enough for me.

I had been shortsighted, selfish, and greedy even in trying to raise money for a worthy purpose. I changed my perspective, and my attitude quickly followed. Instead of thinking merely in dollar amounts, I saw just how much we'd been given already.

Friends had given up their Saturday to help set up and break down the yard sale. It had been in the upper nineties that day, and we had worked on an asphalt surface with very little shade. It was hot and extremely uncomfortable, yet they came anyway to show their love and support for us.

Dozens of people we barely knew from church dropped off their unneeded possessions all week for us to sell. They could have saved their items for their own yard sales, sold them on Craigslist, or kept them in the attic just in case. But they didn't; they gave them to us for Mareto's adoption.

People came to browse the yard sale, and some, not finding anything they wanted to purchase, still stopped by our little cashier's table to drop a few dollars in our donation jar and wish us luck. They had never met us and they didn't know our story, but they were still willing to give.

We'd been given far more than I had realized at first. We'd been given love and sacrifice that we didn't deserve and weren't owed. This realization shifted my heart and gave me a new perspective going into the second yard sale that Saturday.

The weather was still blistering hot, and our friends still showed up to help. I didn't worry about people trying to haggle with me over the prices of various items. I didn't wring my hands and hope that we made "enough." I just worked hard, side by side with my husband and friends, choosing to be grateful for every dollar added to our funds.

About midmorning an old beat-up station wagon pulled into the parking lot. Two parents and three children piled out of the car, and I noticed right away that the baby hadn't been in a car seat. They looked tired, hot, and hungry. I watched for a few moments as they looked around until their eyes settled on the car seat for sale at a nearby table.

My friend met them, exchanged a few words I couldn't hear, and then walked to their vehicle with the car seat in hand to help them install it. Without knowing what was said, I knew exactly what was happening. She was giving this family the car seat for free. The next thing I knew, we all sprang into action.

A couple of friends and I gathered up some children's clothing that looked to be the right sizes and filled a few grocery bags with them. The girls at the bake sale table handed the children cups of ice-cold lemonade and refilled them upon request. We loaded up the back of that family's car with items we thought would be helpful, then watched as they gratefully buckled their baby into her new car seat. My heart swelled with pride as the youth group girls handed them a few bags of cookies just before they drove off, thanking us profusely.

It is better to give than to receive. Those words rang beautifully true that morning.

When the yard sale came to a close, we counted the money we'd collected that morning over the now-lukewarm lemonade. I was shocked to find that the total surpassed the expectations I had hoped for the previous week. It didn't make sense. We hadn't been any busier, I hadn't haggled over prices, and we had given away quite a few of the items.

I don't understand God's math, but I do know that he is in the business of multiplying and adding, not dividing and subtracting. And he knows the intentions of our hearts.

We didn't give the car seat, clothes, toys, and refreshments to that family so that we would get something in return. We did it because it was the loving and right thing to do. And God turned our small yet sincere gift into an even greater one.

Love multiplies, provides, and creates community. We need each other, and we can never lose by choosing to give our love away.

I think back often to Mareto and Arsema bouncing through the living room, tossing imaginary gold dust in the air. I close my eyes and hear their sweet giggles and excited voices. And then I see Mareto refilling his sister's hands from his own supply. The laughter and bouncing and joy continue when the two of them are together.

I DON'T UNDERSTAND GOD'S MATH, BUT I DO KNOW THAT HE IS IN THE BUSINESS OF MULTIPLYING AND ADDING, NOT DIVIDING AND SUBTRACTING.

We need others to love and to add love to our lives. It can be scary letting new people in, but there is so much joy to be found in community and doing life together. No, love doesn't divide and subtract—it multiplies and adds.

seven

"Hi, I Nato!"

Their laughter pierced the air and cut straight to my heart.
It was the sound of several girls, about eight or nine years
old, making fun of a little boy. My little boy. The Mama Bear
inside of me began to growl, and I glared darts right at that
group of laughing girls. It didn't much matter since they
weren't looking in my direction.

They were focused on Mareto, who had noticed the girls
and become curious. He'd run to pay closer attention to them,
but he had gotten distracted by the mulch on the ground and
bent to pick it up. As he reached out his shirt rode up his back,
and the top of his diaper peeked out above the waistband of
his shorts. The girls noticed.

Their laughter was only interrupted by their even louder
exclamations to each other. "Look! That kid is wearing a
diaper!"

I was furious. Mareto heard their laughter and didn't understand it was at his expense, so he popped his head up and smiled. Then he took a few steps toward the girls, stood before them tall and happy, and said, "Hi, I Nato!"

I stayed in the background watching the exchange. The girls grew quiet and curious. They watched him and then noticed me. They smiled a few times, tried to understand his excited chatter, and then eventually moved on to play a game of hide-and-seek. Mareto was content to dig in the mulch and play on the slide with his sister.

I've thought a lot about that exchange, about Mareto's brave response and how it immediately shut down the girls' teasing. I've thought about his innocence and sweetness and how relieved I was that he didn't know they were making fun of him. And I've thought a lot about their reaction . . . and mine.

My first response was protective anger—natural for a mother, I suppose. I was ripping those girls a new one in my head and hoping they caught my glares. But I know how girls are at that age because I was one once myself. A parent's scolding would have only made them angry, and they would have walked away to continue their teasing in private—their words growing harsher as they made each other laugh.

But when Mareto simply introduced himself with kindness and a smile, the girls were baffled. It was clearly not what they expected, and the element of surprise led to curiosity. Their mean laughter transformed into confused but genuine smiles of interest. I could tell they knew Mareto was different, and that they felt a little guilty when they eventually walked away. But I could also tell they sort of liked him.

That's what love does in the face of cruelty. It surprises, confuses, and then teaches.

Mareto's innocence makes him incredibly brave and loving, and the differences between him and other children give him endless opportunities to display that love. Mareto assumes the best of others and doesn't expect to be hurt.

THAT'S WHAT LOVE DOES IN THE FACE OF CRUELTY. IT SURPRISES, CONFUSES, AND THEN TEACHES.

I still remember the evening at church when I first realized that even small children can be harsh to their peers. It was the week before Christmas, and Mareto was three years old. His Awana class was building gingerbread houses, a project intended to be very easy for the children.

A small cardboard house was given to each of the kids, along with their supplies: graham crackers, frosting, a plastic knife, and various bowls of candy. All they had to do was spread some frosting on the cardboard house, place the crackers over that, spread more frosting around, and plop candy on top. Easy. Well . . . easy for everyone else.

Mareto's struggles started before the project even began. The teacher stood at the front and explained the directions. Mareto didn't understand a word of it. I knelt by his chair and whispered the first step to him: "Let's spread some frosting on the house, buddy!"

He looked at me, confused but interested, as I scooped some frosting out of the can with his knife. I handed it to him, but he didn't know what to do with it. So I did what comes naturally for us as a team: I placed my hand over his and manually guided him through the task. A little while later the goopy frosting was dripping from the house.

"Next we need to stick the crackers to the walls and roof. Let's do it together, Mareto!" Then he and I stuck crackers on the house.

I glanced around to see that the other children in class were already placing candy on their houses and decorating them just so. They had all completed their houses without assistance, other than when the teacher reminded them to put the candy on their houses and not in their mouths.

"Okay, it's time to do the frosting again. Do you remember how we did it before?" Mareto shook his head, and we started over—my hand over his, guiding the knife as it spread frosting over the crackers.

The last step was easy. I encouraged him enthusiastically, "This is the best part, Mareto! You can stick candy anywhere on this house! Go crazy!"

He grinned and reached for some gumdrops. A minute later he sat back, satisfied. There were about twelve red gumdrops all on one side of the roof.

"Is that all you want, Mareto? Do you want to put some other candy on the rest of the house?"

He shook his head, so I gushed over his house, telling him how beautiful it looked and how he'd done a great job. He was proud, and it was a sweet little Christmas memory shared by the two of us.

Until the little girl across the table spoke up. "Why is he so dumb?"

The words hung in the air over the table as I stared back, trying to process what this little blonde-haired three-year-old girl had just asked me. Somehow I stammered out, "Ww-what?"

"Why is he so dumb?" she repeated, giving Mareto a look that I can only describe as a mixture of pity and disgust. I was stunned.

I finally stammered out that he simply made his house the way he liked it, and that certain tasks are harder for him than they are for other children—but that he is not dumb at all.

She grew tired of the conversation and went back to rearranging the candies on her roof.

When I looked down at Mareto, there was a golf ball–sized lump in my throat—but he was smiling across the table at the little girl who had just called him dumb. He looked at her little gingerbread house, then back up at her, and said, "Pretty!"

She smiled back and said, "Thanks! I like yours too."

I still cried later that night after I tucked Mareto into bed, but somehow I knew he was going to be okay. The world might not always be kind to him, but he would be kind to the world . . . and teach everyone what love looks like.

I want to be more like Mareto.

My first instinct in the face of meanness isn't love; it's

self-defense. And sometimes self-defense looks a bit like hurting someone else the way they've hurt us, doesn't it? The process usually entails someone hurting me, me hurting them, and both of us walking away angry, resentful, bitter, and maybe a bit ashamed.

When the harried mother accidently cuts us off in traffic because she's late to the doctor, we honk and wave our arms in frustration. Maybe she rushes into the doctor's office feeling mad because some jerk on the road honked and yelled at her, so when the secretary tells her that the appointments are running about forty-five minutes behind, this mom sits in the waiting room, steaming. When she finally gets to see the doctor, she's angry and lets him know. An hour later the frustrated doctor walks into a room and isn't as kind and gentle and compassionate as he should be when he delivers a crushing diagnosis to the parents waiting with fear in their eyes.

Do you see the cycle? Hurt keeps on filtering through everyone until someone stops it. Someone has to be brave enough, or innocent enough, to swallow his or her pride and respond in love. Love changes the trajectory of life.

I believe this is what Jesus was talking about when he said that the greatest commandment of all is to love God with all our heart, soul, and mind, and the second greatest commandment is to love everyone around us as much as we love ourselves. He finished by saying that everything—the law and all the prophets—hinges on us loving God and loving each other.

The world is held together by love. And if that's true, then the opposite is also true: The world falls apart when we don't love God and each other. This is why love wins.

Notice your reaction the next time someone is rude or cruel toward you or someone you love. Is it to respond in kind? When I think back to that day at the playground and the girls who laughed at my son, I know in my heart that my initial reaction was caused by my hurt and anger. I wanted them to see me, and I wanted them to know that they were wrong and to feel ashamed.

Now notice your reaction when someone does something loving and kind toward you or someone you love. Isn't it also easier to respond in kind?

The other week I was navigating a poorly planned parking lot, trying to get to the drive-through line for Starbucks before an appointment. I was in a rush and zipped around a corner, and just as I entered the line, I saw a car in the corner of my eye jolt to a stop. I realized that I had inadvertently cut this woman off because I didn't notice that she had the right of way.

As I glanced in my rearview mirror I saw her waving her hands around, and I could tell she was telling me off to her steering wheel. At first I felt a twinge of guilt, and then I felt frustrated that she was so mad at me when it was an honest mistake. I felt bad, but she didn't know that. For all she knew I was just some entitled brat who couldn't wait an extra five seconds for her fancy coffee. Maybe she was already having a bad day, or maybe not—but I really didn't want to be the cause of it. So I pulled through to the window and told the barista that I wanted to pay for both me and the woman (whom I had just cut off in the parking lot) ordering behind me. Mareto taught me to love like that.

Jesus tells us to love our enemies and pray for those who hurt us. He knows love holds the world together, so it makes sense that we should love the ones who are cruel to us. It is countercultural and goes against our instincts, but loving our enemies is the only way to make wrongs right and darkness light.

Have you ever heard the phrase "Hurt people hurt people"? Though it's true that there are people in the world with evil in their hearts beyond comprehension, most of the "enemies" we come across in our daily lives are simply people who have been hurt. Isn't it funny how we expect so much grace and love from others, yet we resist giving grace and love? I think it's because we know our own stories. We know our hurts and struggles and sacrifices. We don't know other people's stories, so we don't view them with the same eyes we view ourselves.

My husband was a freshman in high school when an older boy named Jimmy "stole" his girlfriend and picked on him relentlessly. I don't know all the details (mainly because John can't remember them), but he told me how much he couldn't stand Jimmy because he thought Jimmy was such a jerk. When Jimmy graduated from high school, John said, "Good riddance." So years later, when John got a friend request from Jimmy on Facebook, it was a bit of a shock. The request was followed up with a private message from Jimmy asking for John's forgiveness for the way he acted in high school.

John cried. He shared it with me, and I cried. John responded, and the two became friends, real friends, for the first time. Then, a few months later, Jimmy sent a link to a video. It was a video created by Jimmy's church of him sharing his testimony, and it left John undone.

As it turned out, Jimmy's dad was an alcoholic who beat him, his mom, and his sisters regularly. This is what he went home to every day as a little boy. When Jimmy was twelve years old, his grandfather murdered his grandmother and uncle. And twelve-year-old Jimmy was left to process this, asking why and receiving no answers. Jimmy, too, wished he was dead. And in high school, at the same time John was so angry at Jimmy and hoped to never see him again, Jimmy drove out to the beach with a gun and the intention to kill himself.

But God had other plans. Just before he pulled the trigger, Jimmy cried out to God—and God touched his heart. I don't know all the ins and outs of how life looked for teenage Jimmy after that, but today he has a beautiful wife and two gorgeous children.

Today Jimmy and John are friends, and John wishes he knew back then what he knows now. What Jimmy really needed was love and a friend.

Maybe the people who drive us nuts don't have a story quite as extreme as Jimmy's, but we all have a story. We've all gone through things that we don't broadcast, but we hold our hurt inside and let it impact how we relate to others.

Maybe the girls who laughed at Mareto had been laughed at and bullied themselves. Maybe they figured the only way to avoid being teased was to be the ones who teased. We know that's not right, but aren't we all just broken people trying to figure out how to do life right?

WE DON'T HAVE TO KNOW SOMEONE'S STORY TO LOVE THEM WELL.

We don't have to know someone's story to love them well. It should be enough to remember that they have a story, just as we do.

Hurt people hurt people. And we're all hurting. There's only one answer that can break the cycle: love. Love holds us together, heals wounds, restores relationships, and changes things. The whole world hinges on us responding in love.

eight

"Aww, That's So Nice"

It's a random Tuesday afternoon, and I lean over in the kitchen to give Mareto a hug. Before straightening back up, I put my face in front of his and say, "I love you."

Mareto smiles, leans in, and says, "Awww, that's so nice."

It sounds like getting rejected on a TV sitcom. You know, when the guy says, "I love you," and the girl responds with, "Oh, wow," and a pat on the back. Sort of like the episode of *Friends* when Ross tells Emily he loves her at the airport and she says, "Thank you." Or in season eight when Ross tells Mona he loves her and she says, "And I like spending time with you!" (Seems like Ross might have some issues, but that's beside the point.)

The point is, when we tell someone, "I love you," the most expected response is, "I love you too." At least, it's the response we hope for. Though Mareto often does respond with his own version of that—which usually sounds something like "I you, too, love you"—he usually responds with, "Aww, that's so nice." And I love it.

I wish I had a way to insert a video of Mareto saying this phrase, because all the feelings that accompany it are wrapped up in the sounds he makes, the expression on his face, and his body language. When Mareto says, "Aww, that's so nice," he isn't awkwardly brushing off my love. He's telling me exactly how he feels.

What he's really saying is, "I heard you tell me you love me, and I believe you. I understand that you love me. I accepted that love, I internalized it, and now I feel so good inside because I feel your love."

I'll tell you what he doesn't do. He doesn't look up at me with skepticism in his eyes and say, "But I didn't share with my sister yesterday." Or, "Yeah, but I said that naughty word you don't like this morning." Or, "I know, but I pitched an enormous tantrum when you wouldn't let me open my Cheez-Its bag on my own today."

Mareto doesn't attach my love to his actions. He hasn't associated his behavior with how I feel about him, nor should he, because, as any parent knows, the one has absolutely nothing to do with the other.

So why do we approach God or each other the opposite way? When did we forget that we don't have to earn God's love, because we already have it? When did we stop relating to each other as human beings? Somewhere between childhood and adulthood we stopped believing that love is something to be accepted—no strings attached.

Several years ago, the church we attended was going through a difficult time. My husband had been working there for more than two years, and the transition hadn't been easy for us or for some of the church members. Just when we thought we were catching our stride, another group of members and churchgoers began to voice their displeasure with nearly all of the church staff in hurtful ways.

That winter I flew out to a conference alone for the first time in my adult life. I walked into the main session feeling exhausted and beaten—already a failure. I had a seventeen-month-old toddler at home with medical issues we couldn't figure out, and a church family who hated us (which wasn't really true, but that's how it felt). My shortcomings had been pointed out to me or whispered about repeatedly for the past two years, so they were at the forefront of my mind.

I almost didn't attend the conference. I thought I would walk away feeling even more condemned than before, feeling that I should be doing more. More of what, I wasn't sure. Just more.

The band started their first set of worship music, and I sang along from the back. They started their second song, and as the first slide popped up on the screen, I did an inward eye-roll. "Oh, How He Loves Us" began, and I confess I was not excited. The song had been played incessantly on my local radio station, and I had gotten in the habit of changing the station whenever it came on. I'd yell at the radio, "There *are* other songs, you know!"

We Christians tend to do this: determine what songs we

want to sing to the Lord in worship, rather than consider that he might want to sing a song over us.

So I stood and closed my eyes, because I knew every word from memory, and sang, "Oh, how he loves us" over and over. Somewhere between the first time we sang that chorus and the fifth time . . . it sank in.

I didn't know I was crying until I felt the tears dripping off my chin. I had no idea I needed to not just be told God loves me, but to believe it. By the time the song ended, I felt such an overwhelming sense of God's love for me. So I did what we all have been tempted to do. I gave God a list of reasons why he shouldn't love me.

"But God, I didn't react so well when my faults were pointed out to me."

I love you.

"But God, I'm not sure I'm doing such a great job at this whole parenting thing. My son is sick, and I can't figure out why."

I love you.

"Last week I screamed at my husband. I'm so ashamed of the way I let my anger get the better of me."

I love you.

"It's been a month since I opened my Bible, and I don't pray like I should. Most of the time I feel like I'm just reading you a list of requests."

I love you.

And somewhere amid this dialogue, I let it sink in that God loves me—and it felt so nice inside. Better than nice. It felt like burdens being lifted, chains being broken, wounds being healed, and brokenness being redeemed. Somewhere along the way I had forgotten that God loves me—no if, ands, or buts about it—and I had started believing that God's love was dependent upon my behavior.

The Bible itself is one great love story between God and his creation, but there's one chapter in particular that gets all the attention when the topic of love is brought up. You've probably seen it stitched on a pillow or heard it read at a wedding. Yes, I'm talking about 1 Corinthians 13.

To me, this passage is as much about receiving love as it is about giving it. One sentence stands out to me: "[Love] is not irritable or resentful" (v.5). The New International Version says, "It keeps no record of wrongs."

We can receive God's love freely and fully, because he isn't holding our actions against us. He isn't resentful of the things we did or didn't do last week or ten minutes ago. God's love isn't contingent on what we bring to the table. It simply *is*.

GOD'S LOVE ISN'T CONTINGENT ON WHAT WE BRING TO THE TABLE. IT SIMPLY *IS*.

It would pain me deeply if Mareto did not want to accept my love. If he pushed it away or thought his own actions made him unworthy of it, I would get down on my knees over and over again and say, "I love you!" until he believed me.

We don't realize how much

we hurt others by brushing away and refusing to accept their expressions of love. Think about the last time someone paid you a really nice compliment. Perhaps another woman commented on your dress or cute shoes. Maybe you responded, "Oh, this old thing? I just picked it up at the thrift store!"

I was recently chatting with a couple of friends about this when someone complimented a pair of shoes I was wearing. I immediately made sure they knew I had gotten a great deal on them—two pairs for twenty dollars! Why did I do that? Because I was uncomfortable just receiving the kind words and loving gesture.

Think about the last time you were given an unexpected, extravagant gift. How did you respond? Maybe you said something along the lines of, "Oh, you shouldn't have!" or "I can't accept this!"

Of course you can accept it. This person went out of their way to show their love for you because they wanted to, and because it brings them joy to express their love for you. But when you reject it or brush it off or explain it away, you're essentially saying, "I don't deserve this." As if you were supposed to.

Why do we pain God's heart by trying to earn his love?

We have a distorted understanding of love. We watch too many movies and TV shows and let our own baggage cloud our view. We see a culture that has grown comfortable with falling in and out of love and changing partners faster than we change vehicles. And we've attached the label of "love" to things that aren't love.

Love isn't a feeling. Love is a fact.

I've heard a lot about love being a choice, that we choose to love others, and I believe that's true. But I also believe that some love is an unwavering fact. We might not always choose to act in a loving manner toward others, but the fact of our love can still remain.

I might not respond well to Mareto saying a naughty word for the fourteenth time one day. I might lose my patience and be less than gracious. But my love for him remains a fact, even though I didn't choose the best way to respond to his behavior.

I might be low on sleep, with dishes and laundry piling up, and when my husband comes home after a long day of work I might be short with him. It's not a very loving way to treat him in the moment, but the fact of my love for him still remains.

We may not always act lovely, but we still can love and be loved.

And the best part is that God doesn't mess up the way we do. Not only does he never waver in his love for us, but he always acts out of that love, no matter our behavior. The even better part is that God doesn't love us in spite of who we are. God loves us for who we are. God created us as reflections of his beauty and because he wanted to have a relationship with each one of us.

God isn't waiting for us to clean up our act. He isn't waiting for us to deserve his love or try hard enough to earn it. He's begging us to accept his love right now, as we are.

Have you been cranky and rude lately? God loves you.

Did you yell at your kids this morning? God loves you.

Did you shoplift as a teenager (or yesterday)? God loves you.

Have you cheated or lied? God loves you.

Did you hurt somebody you love? God loves you.

Have you been the bully? God loves you.

Are you arrogant, boastful, or conceited? God loves you.

Do you lust over your friend's spouse? God loves you.

Are you greedy and terrible with money? God loves you.

Are you more focused on material things than spiritual things? God loves you.

Do you hate yourself? God loves you.

Maybe you have screwed your life up so badly you can't see any light or love left in it. Maybe that's where you're sitting today, feeling lower and more rotten than ever before. "But God shows his love for us in that while we were still sinners, Christ died for us" (Romans 5:8).

We didn't earn it. We don't deserve it.

God is simply saying, "I love you." And the best way to respond is by believing him, accepting his love, internalizing it, and saying, "Aww, that's so nice."

nine

"Look! The Tree Rainbow!"

Mareto loves light and color. He is especially excited by rainbows. One day I was switching out a CD, and he noticed the way the underside caught the light and reflected a rainbow. He begged to hold it and spent the next couple of hours carrying it through the house with his little index finger poked through the center hole. He twisted and turned it at different angles, tilting his head to look at the rainbow. Mareto finds light and color in the ordinary.

One day we were walking through the woods when Mareto stopped abruptly and looked up to exclaim, "Look! The tree rainbow!" I followed his gaze toward a tree that was bent and partially fallen. Its skinny trunk grew up out of the dirt and then arched over a pathway, where it ended by resting on a tree several feet away. It was tall, bending high above us, and creating a shape in the sky just like a rainbow. And I never would have noticed it.

But Mareto did. Mareto sees beauty in places I wouldn't expect to find it, such as the broken trunk of a tree.

We kept walking, and not too many minutes passed before Mareto stooped to pick up a small, dirty, gray rock. He turned it over in the palm of his hand a few times before holding it up to show me. "The rock is a heart!" he exclaimed with bright, wide eyes, barely holding in his awe and excitement. Sure enough, this small rock looked as if it had been crudely cut into the shape of a heart. I wouldn't have noticed that either.

Mareto's eyes seem trained to find the beauty in everything. I remember a time when mine were, too, but somewhere along the way, I lost it.

I remember trotting through the woods with my sister as a child, looking for acorns to collect, then popping their tops off and pretending they were tiny bowls for tiny animals. I remember inspecting each rock, hoping to discover an old arrowhead. I remember lying in the grass to braid clover flowers together for necklaces and bracelets. I remember finding shapes in the clouds and dancing in the rain.

When did I lose my vision?

Life got hard and big and scary. The world no longer felt or looked beautiful; instead it seemed broken and messy and ugly. I stopped finding beauty in everything because I was too focused on the brokenness. Terrible things happen and we can't always control them, so a narrative of fear writes itself in our hearts—scribbling out the story of broken beauty, but beauty nonetheless.

I was in kindergarten when the neighbor's house burned to the ground. We walked by it on our way to the bus stop, and I can still see the charred, black bones of the house poking up out of the ash heaps. It was eerie and icky and ugly. Seeing the ashes of what used to be someone's home sparked fear and sadness in me.

Today the smell of smoke doesn't fill me with excitement for bonfires and s'mores; it makes me nauseous. Watching flames dance and flicker against a black night sky doesn't relax and warm me. Instead, I feel tense and anxious. I have forgotten to focus on the beauty of the flame and instead have tuned my gaze to the destruction it can bring.

My siblings and I spent most of our childhood outdoors. We filled our weekends with trips to the beach or the mountains, either swimming in the ocean and playing among the kelp or hiking the switchback trails in the mountains of California. I loved it, and my memories of a childhood spent in places like La Jolla, Del Mar, Yosemite, and Mount Palomar are amazing.

But I lost perspective.

One day we were hiking to some waterfalls, and we wanted to picnic across a river that was, in my childhood memory, deep and raging. There were some large rocks that served as stepping-stones, but there was no bridge. Because my brother was a toddler, my father's plan was to carry him over the rocks and the rest of us would go one by one. I watched as my dad's foot slipped and his hiking boot dipped into the water before he caught himself and made it to the other side.

But my mind couldn't stop there. The reel playing in my head carried the fall all the way through, and I envisioned my dad crashing into the river and my toddler brother being swept away in the current, unable to swim and save himself. I was terrified. I think hiking changed for me that day.

Suddenly I saw danger everywhere. Instead of taking in the gorgeous views of the Grand Canyon, I worried that my brother would tumble over the edge. Instead of feeling the anticipation of a beautiful panoramic view as we climbed switchbacks, I worried about rattlers in the bushes. Instead of enjoying gorgeous and refreshing waterfalls, I worried about bee stings and bugs. Instead of marveling at the sunset over the mountain, I worried about the distant howls of coyotes.

Then I entered fifth grade, and two madmen in Oklahoma blew up a building. Images flashed across TV screens and newspaper covers. Kids in school chattered on the playground about what they were hearing on the radio and in their homes, and I was scared. I went to the skating rink in our new Windstar minivan and worried that the rink would be bombed. Nothing felt safe anymore. Even now, when I smell that new-car smell, I think of 1995 and shattered buildings and broken bodies.

My tendency to lean into brokenness has carried into adulthood. Honestly, it's justifiable—because the truth is, our world is a terribly broken place. Many days I avoid the news for fear of walking around with a cloud over my head for the rest of the day. But I've learned in an unexpected way that hiding just above those threatening clouds can be something incredible.

I look above the clouds every time I get on an airplane. I absolutely hate flying. I hate my nerves, the anxiety that creeps in, the turbulence . . . all of it. But there is one moment I look forward to every time I am forced to get on a plane. It happens just a few minutes after takeoff (which is my least favorite part of a flight).

A couple of years ago, that moment couldn't come fast enough for me. John pulled up to the curb at the airport, and I exited the passenger side with my face tilted skyward. Dark, low clouds hovered above, and the wind whipped my hair into my face. My palms sweated as I wondered if my plane would even take off that morning.

I kissed John good-bye, and he whispered, "It's going to be fine!" into my ear as we shared one more hug. I made my way through the airport to my gate and discovered my flight would be leaving early. The lady at the desk explained that we were under a thunderstorm warning, and the pilot wanted to get in the air as soon as possible to beat the storm.

As our plane zoomed down the runway, my heart pounded in my chest. The wheels lifted, and we were airborne, climbing upward and into those angry, dark storms. Suddenly I lost all visibility as we entered a layer of cloud cover. The plane shook and rumbled, and we kept climbing. My hands gripped the armrests of my seat, and I focused on taking deep breaths.

Then it happened.

As I kept my eyes fixed on the window, it suddenly flashed bright white. The plane broke through the thick layer of haze, and I stared out at the wide expanse of the bright blue sky and cotton-ball clouds below. The sun beamed, and the plane soared steadily—with no evidence of the thunderstorm brewing on the ground below.

Beauty is there, always. Beauty and peace and hope are hiding right around the corner (or just above the clouds). And sometimes beauty is hiding in plain sight, right there in the broken; we just have to train our eyes to see it.

In her heartbreaking book about losing her daughter in a tragic accident, Mary Beth Chapman expresses this truth about the coexistence of beauty and brokenness: "If we keep our heads down, either out of defeat or loss or shame or tiredness . . . whatever the reason, we are going to miss the beautiful sun (and Son) that is right there in front of us, shining its warmth on our faces and our souls!"[1]

This world is fallen and therefore broken. We exist in brokenness. But that doesn't mean we exist without hope and joy and light and life. We were not created for evil. We

> SOMETIMES BEAUTY IS HIDING IN PLAIN SIGHT, RIGHT THERE IN THE BROKEN; WE JUST HAVE TO TRAIN OUR EYES TO SEE IT.

were not created to be permanently broken. We were not created to live a mundane and meaningless existence, and that is where the beauty lies.

We were created in the image of a perfect God, to reflect wholeness and courage and faith and grace. We were created to shine our own light like a beacon, illuminating the beauty we find around us.

Our family was born out of brokenness. This acknowledgment makes some people uncomfortable, but it's entirely true. Our family is the result of broken hearts and broken stories. And our family is beautiful.

As much as adoption reflects the heart of God to his children, it also reflects the brokenness of humanity and our initial rejection of God. If sin and death and destruction had never entered the world, we never would have needed Jesus to die for us on the cross. That initial fall—the loss, the separation, and turning away from our Father—broke his heart. It wasn't God's best for us, and it hurt everyone: both God and his children. Jesus was God's answer to that brokenness. And his death and resurrection were excruciatingly beautiful.

Have you ever seen the film *The Passion of the Christ*? It's the full story of our adoption into the family of God, and when the closing credits scrolled, I flipped the hood of my sweatshirt up over my head so the people outside the theater wouldn't see my swollen red eyes and blotchy face. Why? Because that story is glorious and messy and agonizing. It's the complete picture.

John and I lost so much on our way to building a family,

and my children lost even more. But our story is such a blend of the broken and the beautiful. I recently felt prompted to write my children a letter that I hope brings them peace and validation as they grow up. I wanted to share the broken parts of my story, mirrored by the broken parts of their stories, and then show how we get to take our jagged pieces and fit them together to create something painfully lovely.

We didn't choose this. You and I. We didn't pick this story.

I didn't choose the months and years of heartache, pain, broken dreams, and dashed hopes.

I didn't choose the monthly roller coaster ride of hope, anticipation, and crushing disappointment and defeat.

I didn't choose the nights of crying myself to sleep.

I didn't choose the tests, procedures, and never-ending doctor appointments.

I didn't choose the pile of bills sitting next to my fertility books.

I didn't choose the phone call we got when I was just twenty-four, telling me that my dreams of carrying a child simply couldn't come true.

I didn't choose that road of pain ... of infertility and loss.

You didn't choose this.

You didn't choose the weeks and months and maybe lifetime of pain and fear and loss and trauma.

You didn't choose to lose everything you knew ... your home, culture, family.

You didn't choose to leave the familiar smells, sounds, and sights of your country.

You didn't choose the nights of crying yourself to sleep.

You didn't choose the illness, the hospital visits, the fear.

You didn't choose the phone call we got telling us your life would be forever changed.

You didn't choose that road of pain . . . of relinquishment and loss.

But . . .

I choose you. I choose all of you. I choose your heart and your spirit and your life.

I choose to see you. All of you.

I choose to cry with you and hold you when the nights are hard and sleep won't come.

I choose days filled with laughter and tears. Hard questions and answers that are difficult to find.

I choose to be with you amid every high and every low. The good things and the hard things.

I choose us. I choose our love, our family, and our life together. I choose redemption and healing and grace, in all its wondrous and painful and messy ways.

We didn't get to choose the past, but I choose to create our future together. With you. Every minute, every hour . . . I choose you. I choose you yesterday, today, and always. I want to be with you. I love you.

God tells us that when we love him, "all things work together for good" (Romans 8:28). That doesn't mean everything that happens to us will *be* good; it means that God is bigger than our suffering and the world's suffering. It means that God is actually powerful enough to make something lovely in spite of and out of the messiest and most awful parts of life.

But do we see it? Do we look for the beauty hiding around the next corner?

Do we actually see the arc of a rainbow or just the broken trunk of a tree? Do we believe the sun is beaming above the dark clouds, or do we fixate on the storm? Do we see that every single broken thing in life is really just redemption waiting to happen?

I don't always see the beauty. I admit that it's not always my first inclination. I spent so many years seeing the broken in the world that it takes a conscious effort to look for the good in the bad. But Mareto is helping me—taking my hand and showing me all the beautiful things in this world—and I'm watching him live it out.

Mareto reminds me that a moment of insult is an opportunity to forgive. A friend in trouble is a chance to help. Loss is a reminder of heaven, and pain pushes us to our Helper. There is beauty and light in everything. We simply need to train our eyes to find it.

ten

"I Smell Jellyfish!"

Mareto knows how to laugh. I mean, *really* laugh. He isn't self-conscious or serious or reserved. When something tickles him he just lets it go. Laughter rumbles deep in his belly and bubbles up and out of his wide-open mouth in the form of big hoots, giggles, and hiccups. Mareto perfectly embodies the term *belly laugh*.

And it's contagious.

He and Arsema have a little game that I don't understand. I have no idea where it originated or why it's funny, but they love it. It will start in a quiet moment in the living room. Mareto will be sitting on the couch arranging his toys on the coffee table. Arsema will be on her knees on the carpet with her dolls and ice cream shop toy, playing restaurant in her little singsongy voice. It's peaceful and serene, and I go to brew a cup of tea. Then, out of nowhere, Mareto pipes up . . .

"I smell jellyfish!"

Arsema immediately snaps her head upward, eyes lighting up, and while the word *jellyfish* is just barely leaving Mareto's mouth, she shouts her part.

"NO jellyfish!"

And they both dissolve into a fit of laughter. I don't get it. It's utter nonsense to me. Yet there I am, listening in the kitchen and giggling to myself. Joy is contagious that way.

I'm not in on the joke, and to be perfectly honest, I don't know if Arsema and Mareto even know what the joke is. I think they just happened upon this little game by accident. Maybe Mareto smelled something odd one day, and in his mind he decided it was jellyfish. And maybe Arsema was a little annoyed and responded with, "No jellyfish!" quite seriously, but once the exchange happened, they both thought it sounded a little funny. So a game was born, and it pops up without warning and results in big, hiccupping belly laughs.

Along the way, we adults often lose that sense of fun. Life gets serious, and we forget how to be silly and laugh without reserve. When big worries get in the way, it becomes harder to uncover the laughter waiting in our bellies. We forget to play, because big important work is looming over us and the concerns of life weigh on our spirits and push the laughter further down.

But it's there, waiting in our bellies to be let out. And it needs to be let out. We often claim we don't have time for fun or play or laughter, because there is work to be done and bills to be paid and people to disciple and dinner to be cooked. But the truth is, sometimes the most important work is laughter.

Did you know there is a thing called "play therapy"? Yes, this is an actual discipline in the mental health community, and it is highly regarded. It is mainly used with children, but I think we all could probably benefit from a little play therapy. It's been around since the early twentieth century but has gained momentum in the last twenty years or so.

SOMETIMES THE MOST IMPORTANT WORK IS LAUGHTER.

Charles Schaefer, who is considered the father of play therapy, observed that play is as important to our happiness as love and work. Play (laughter and joy and silliness) is just as crucial to our health and well-being as giving and receiving love and the productivity and fulfillment of a job well done.

The role of play in our lives is bigger than we adults care to imagine. In fact, according to Garry Landreth, the author of *Play Therapy: The Art of the Relationship*, it's critical to a full, well-rounded, meaningful life. The title of his book alone suggests how important the role of play is to our connection with others. Landreth describes it as a fun, enjoyable activity that elevates our spirits and brightens our outlook on life. It expands self-expression, self-knowledge, self-actualization, and self-efficacy. Play relieves feelings of stress and boredom, connects us to people in a positive way, stimulates creative thinking and exploration, regulates our emotions, and boosts our confidence.

I first learned about play therapy after Mareto came home and I was working to build a strong and healthy attachment with him. We had missed out on being together during the first months of his life, when foundations are usually laid for a healthy relationship, so I wanted to do all I could to secure a strong connection with my son. I was delighted to find that one of the best ways I could do this was simply to play with him.

Our play has changed and advanced over the years, of course. In the baby months I would sometimes set him on the floor in his Bumbo seat and stare at him. How does one play with a drooling baby who hasn't yet figured out how to sit up on his own? It's not as though we could build Lego towers or train tracks together. But then I'd make a silly face or nuzzle my nose in his neck fat, and he'd giggle. Thus we created our own play. I learned what made him laugh, and I'd do it until he got bored or I got tired.

One evening when Mareto was close to a year old, I heard screaming fits of laughter coming down the hall. I was washing dishes, and John was giving Mareto a bath. He had obviously discovered a new game. I peeked around the corner to see what was so funny. John was simply scooping water into a cup, holding it high above Mareto's head, and then tipping the cup to pour the water back into the tub right into Mareto's lap. And Mareto couldn't handle the hilarity of it.

It wasn't belly laughs coming out of Mareto that evening; it was loud, shrieking laughter. John had to take breaks because Mareto was losing his breath. And it went on for a while. I'm so glad I had time to grab my phone and record a couple minutes of this delight. Just like the jellyfish game, it was utter nonsense—but John and I were cracking up because joy is contagious.

I can't pinpoint for you exactly when or how we started building such a strong bond and healthy attachment with our children. I don't think it was one moment of play or one night of working through tears and bad dreams. I think it was likely a combination of several things, not the least of which was God's grace to our family. But I can tell you that our relationship became both strong and beautiful.

My husband says that human beings were created for relationship. He's preached entire sermons on the topic. We were never meant to live and work and cry and laugh alone. We need other people in our lives. We need deep and meaningful connections to experience fulfillment and joy.

Laughing together, being silly and ridiculous, making up our own games, and creating inside jokes with our friends, spouses, and siblings is some of the best stuff of life. And it is as foundational to healthy bonds as crying and grieving and mourning and suffering and walking through the hardest moments of life.

We tend to prefer either/or thinking to complexity. Maybe it's easier for us to view life as black and white and not so gray. We want the guidebook to be super clear—always turn left at the fork in the road and right at the T—but life is more often both/and. And it's a whole lot more rainbow-colored than monochromatic.

So when it comes to meaningful, rich living, we need to

embrace both tears *and* laughter. And we usually need to do it at the same time.

As I've already mentioned, my grandmother, Grammy, passed away last fall. My mom called one morning to tell me, and I sat on the bottom step of our stairwell and cried. The kids came over, a little amazed by my tears, and sat next to me. Arsema rubbed my back while Mareto hugged me and gave his usual sweet, "It's okay about it! Are you sad, Mommy? It's okay about it!"

I spent the whole day thinking about Grammy—how much I loved her and how wonderful a grandmother she'd been. I thought about how much I had learned from her about life. How can we only fully understand what other people have taught us after they're gone? I wish I'd focused a little more on that while she was still alive.

Later that day I sat down at the computer to process my thoughts and feelings and what I wanted to tell the world about my Grammy. I ended up reading what I wrote that day at her memorial service:

Grammy is my second grandparent to move on to heaven, and I realize it's such a gift that I made it so far into adulthood with all four of my grandparents. Of course the other side of that coin is that it hurts that much more to lose someone who has loved and cheered for you for so many years.

When my mom called to tell me that Grammy had passed away, it brought back a flood of memories.

I've looked through some pictures, yes, but mostly I've searched the catalog of memories in my heart and simply sat with them.

There's a unique mix of snapshots in my mind. For instance, I remember sitting on the steps in her old home after she hung up the phone with her daughter Jody. I caught her wiping tears from her cheeks. When I asked her why she was crying, she said, "Oh, honey. It's so hard to have a sick baby." My cousin Nicholas passed away from a long battle with cancer years later. I don't know why, but this picture of her grieving for her grandson has always been vivid in my mind.

And I remember waking up and padding into her kitchen for her to make me some "dippy eggs" (her term for over easy . . . because we could dip our toast in the yolk). I remember the rows of jars filled with homemade applesauce in her pantry. I remember her scrubbing us when we were little in the bath and checking behind our ears to make sure she got every single speck of dirt off us.

But the image most ingrained in my heart is of her laughing. Grammy laughed a lot. When I think of her, the face that first pops into my mind is her laughing face. She laughed with us, she laughed at my Pap, she laughed at her kids, and she laughed at all of our stories. She was an incredible sport about everything—which I suppose was necessary with three rambunctious boys—and seemed to really experience joy even though life wasn't always easy.

It's caused me to think about how I want my children (and hopefully someday grandchildren) to remember me when my time on earth is over. I truly hope the image that pops into their minds first is my face with a wide-open smile and eyes crinkled in laughter. I want to spend my life loving, and laughing, well. Because that's what Grammy did and it's how I'll always remember her.

My grandmother had her struggles in life, and I don't know the half of them. But she also knew how to laugh. My father shared his message of love for his mom shortly after I spoke, and I was touched by the reaction of everyone listening in the church. He cried and we cried as he told of her dedication to her family and work, and of her unfailing love for others. Then we all laughed as he told stories of his youth and the things that made her unique and wonderful. There we were, remembering a life with tears and laughter.

Yes, our tears bound us in a shared loss, but even more so, I think our laughter connected us to Grammy and to each other. Because suddenly I realized we were a family rich with inside jokes. Stories were told throughout the day that we all knew and had heard a hundred times, and our sides still split with laughter.

It would start with a story from my dad. Then when the laughter died down, someone else would pipe up, "Remember that one time . . ." And off we'd go again, laughing and nodding. On and on it went.

Connecting through laughter is contagious.

The Bible says there is "a time to weep, and a time to laugh; a time to mourn, and a time to dance" (Ecclesiastes 3:4).

We don't always recognize that it's the same time. And it's right now.

This has been made so apparent to me during the annual Created for Care Retreats, when nine hundred adoptive and foster mothers come to Georgia for love, encouragement, and equipment. Some of these women work tirelessly every day, trying to help their children and families heal from traumas.

Created for Care offers sessions to equip them with new tools for their parenting belts, but we also want to encourage and have fun with them. Because when you're carrying the heavy parts of life, you really do need laughter too. Not instead of, but in addition to. So what do we, as a team, do? Well, we make fools of ourselves.

One year our founder, Andrea, got on stage in a red wig, moon boots, and a "Vote for Pedro" T-shirt and shocked everyone by doing the entire dance from *Napoleon Dynamite*. Another year we dressed up in full eighties rock gear and lip-synced some Bon Jovi and Journey, then told the audience to come back for a night of karaoke. One year we prancercised our way down the aisles. If you don't know what that is, Google it. You're welcome.

After the eighties rocker performance, two friends came running up to me in shock and delight, saying they just couldn't believe what they were seeing. They kept looking at each other saying, "Is that really Lauren Casper on the drums in a tattoo sleeve with a fake cigarette?"

As much as the ladies loved our shenanigans, though, the team members are the ones who have the most fun. Really. We know we're being absolutely ridiculous, but it makes us laugh. It makes other people laugh, too, and the laughter has led to some really special relationships. Relationships where we can laugh and cry, share and be heard, grow and create.

Laughter is so important. Give yourself a little play therapy. It keeps us sane in a world that seems to be falling off the tracks most days. Laughter relieves our stress, expands our minds, builds our creativity, and strengthens our relationships—so get a little silly today. Smell the jellyfish.

eleven

"Stephen's in Danger!"

In Mareto's world, it can be difficult to distinguish cartoon characters from real-life individuals. I think we can all relate to that. There have been times when I wanted to throw my popcorn bowl at the TV set when something awful happens to one of my favorite characters. Or worse ... he or she gets killed off the show. And we've all probably seen the memes or commercials for Netflix showing aimless people wondering what to do with themselves when their favorite show ends. The point is, we get overly invested in the lives of characters on the screen, and Mareto is no different.

For a long time, his very best friends seemed to be the trains from *Thomas & Friends*, including an old engine named Stephen. In one movie that is on repeat at our house, Stephen wanders into a coal mine. Suddenly there is an avalanche of rocks, and the opening to the mine is completely blocked off. Eventually Stephen's friends notice he is missing and go off to search for him. Meanwhile Stephen is calling for help in the mine, certain that no one will ever find him.

For about a year Mareto would tell everyone he saw, "Stephen's in danger!" His eyes would grow wide with his earnest plea. Stephen was in danger, and we all needed to be aware! Sometimes he would add, "We need to find him!"

Mareto loves Stephen, and when you're loved by Mareto you aren't forgotten or ignored when times get tough. His sweet concern over a fictional character makes me think a lot about real life. How do we react when someone is in trouble? How do we respond to a friend (or stranger) in need? When times get tough for others, do we go out of our way for them, or do we retreat?

Even further, do we get the word out? Do we enlist the help of others when our own efforts aren't enough?

One of the most common things I hear from friends and family when someone they love is going through a tough season or has experienced a tragedy is, "I just feel so helpless." Or, "I want to do something, but I don't know what to do."

I think it's our uncertainty that holds us back rather than a lack of caring, but the key may be just showing up. Show up before you feel ready and before a plan is formed. Show up to make the plan. Show up to demonstrate that you are ready and mobilized for action. Just show up. It's always better to show up than to *not* show up.

Maybe when we create specific "helper" roles, it makes

us think we can leave the helping to those who have chosen those roles for themselves. We have policemen and fire-fighters and nurses and doctors and therapists and teachers and counselors and social workers and pastors and so on to do so much of the helping.

It's ingrained in us to think that certain people are helpers. A popular quote from the beloved Fred Rogers illustrates this: "When I was a boy and I would see scary things in the news, my mother would say to me, 'Look for the helpers. You will always find people who are helping.'"[1] Maybe their existence leaves the rest of us thinking we're off the hook when we don't know what to do because, after all, there are people specially designated for helping others.

That's all well and good for a little while, but who helps the helpers? When they buckle under the weight of carrying the world's burdens, who comes to their aid?

I would like to suggest that we should. Everyday, ordinary people who don't have a special title or qualification next to our names should come to the rescue. Because we're all connected and we need each other—every one of us.

When I was a little girl we went camping at the Redwood National Park. You know that famous tree with the carved-out trunk that you can drive your car right through? We drove our car through it. We hiked among the giant redwoods, and I looked up to see their branches reaching higher than I'd ever seen any tree reach. The Redwood Forest is almost magical. I felt like I'd entered a fairyland where I was shrunk down to a pint-sized pixie in a forest of mammoth trees.

Redwood trees are the tallest trees on earth, reaching more than three hundred feet in height. It would be logical to assume that they also have the deepest root systems on earth in order to support their extreme heights, but they don't. In fact, redwoods have surprisingly shallow roots that only grow about six to twelve feet deep. How, then, do they get support and strength to withstand storms and earthquakes and strong winds?

Instead of driving their roots deep into the ground, the redwood trees extend their roots wide, more than fifty feet out from their trunks. And they live in groves, intertwining their roots with the roots of other redwoods in the grove. In other words, they hold each other up and depend on one another to stand through the tough elements. The tallest tree in the grove is connected to the smallest, and they mutually support each other.

And it's not a simple arrangement of the smallest tree depending on the tallest one's extended roots to stand; the benefit goes both ways. They cannot stand and survive alone. The weakest and the strongest both need each other.

So it is with humans too.

My husband is one of those "designated helpers." As a pastor and chaplain at a military college, he is often on the front lines of tragedy. When he is late coming home from work, or he misses dinner and

THE WEAKEST AND THE STRONGEST BOTH NEED EACH OTHER.

bedtime with the kids, it usually isn't because a meeting ran late or a project is due the next day. It's usually because someone died, got into an accident, or was in immediate need of counseling and comfort.

When tragedy strikes at the school, one of the first phone calls always goes to John. We learned quickly the toll this would take on him and our whole family. About four months after John stepped into the chaplain position, the unthinkable happened. It was a perfect spring evening, and we had just put the kids in the bathtub after finishing dinner. I was getting ready to pick up the toys scattered in the living room when John's cell phone rang in his pocket. I sat next to the tub, watching the kids splash so that he could answer the call. Less than a minute later John popped his head around the corner, uniform already in hand, to inform me, "I've got to go. Sorry."

I stepped into the hall. "What? Can't you just finish giving the kids a bath and help me get them to bed? Can whatever it is just wait another hour?" I was still learning that when John said he had to go, he meant it.

"No, it can't wait. A cadet just committed suicide thirty minutes ago," was his tense response. He finished changing and went to collect his wallet and the car keys. With a quick kiss he was out the door. My mouth was still hanging open in shock.

John didn't come home until the early morning hours. He spent all night informing friends, comforting loved ones, and trying to help in the midst of absolute heartbreak and devastation. He came home exhausted in body and heart. After a short rest, a few hours of sleep, and one hot meal, he was right back in the thick of it.

This is John's job, and he wouldn't do it if he didn't want to. But that doesn't mean it doesn't weigh on him at times, or that his own life runs so smoothly that he's able to give to others so freely.

Because that same night, while I was giving the kids their bath, I felt a small lump on Arsema's chest. It was tiny, but noticeable. I shrugged it off—surely it was nothing. But three weeks later the lump had more than tripled in size and was visibly protruding from her chest.

Concerned, I made an appointment with the pediatrician. We moms have a special gift of assuming the worst. I call it worrying, but my friend calls it "being highly tuned in to the needs of our children." I just wanted the doctor to ease my fears and tell me it was nothing. Maybe a harmless cyst. But she didn't.

After feeling the lump she said with a fair degree of certainty that it wasn't a cyst, because it was solid, not fluid. Then she looked up Arsema's records and noted that she hadn't gained any weight at all in more than eight months—not particularly normal for an almost two-year-old. She asked about sleep, and I told her that Arsema had been waking up a lot with night sweats. We left the office a little while later with a referral to the surgical and oncology office at the nearest children's hospital.

I was terrified. The surgeon scheduled Arsema for

surgery the following week to remove the lump and do a biopsy. He looked me in the eye and said very clearly, "I do not want you to worry about this at all." Yeah, right.

So, while John was ministering to others in the wake of a community-shattering death, planning a funeral, and meeting with hurting friends, he was also coming home to a worried wife, scheduling appointments and surgeries, and trying to hold it all together.

Two weeks later Arsema's surgery was over. Her incision was healing, and the pathology lab called to tell me that the results were benign. Our story resolved in the best possible way, but it doesn't for everyone.

Those few weeks were some of the scariest I've ever known as a mother. Even now, years later, I look back at those weeks and feel a churning in my gut. The weight of the world seemed to be on our shoulders. There was no place to escape the burdens we faced. John went to work and faced a grief-stricken community, coming home with the heaviness of the day etched on his face. But instead of finding relief at home, he would look at our daughter and wonder what the next weeks would hold.

Sorrows don't pass over certain people. We will all face tragedy in our lives at some point, and seasons that feel too overwhelming to bear. We will all face trouble and need others to hold us up through the uncertainty, pain, and grief we'll inevitably face.

Showing up in times of trouble takes on different forms. When a loved one dies, it can look like organizing meals for the family, coming over to take care of the kids, or washing the dishes and folding the laundry. It's organizing fundraisers or starting a prayer vigil. It's running to the store for groceries or taking their car to be serviced. It's mowing the lawn of the young mother whose husband is deployed.

Sometimes showing up is just showing up. It's holding your best friend's baby girl and crying in the corner as she passes into heaven. It's sitting in the hospital waiting room with worried spouses or parents. It's attending a funeral or a prayer vigil. It's sitting in the living room, or hospital room, and just listening.

First Corinthians 12:26 tells us, "If one member suffers, all suffer together; if one member is honored, all rejoice together." If even one of us is hurting, we are all hurting—because we are connected even when we forget. Mother Teresa supposedly said, "If we have no peace it is because we have forgotten we belong to each other." We belong to each other in good times and in bad. We need one another.

Just last year, what started as a typical November evening transformed into something unrecognizable when terrorists stormed into concert halls and cafés and stadiums in Paris with guns firing and bombs exploding. The world looked on in horror, disbelief, and grief. I've never been to France and I knew no one there, but I was shocked and heartbroken all the same—because I don't need to know my brothers and sisters personally to care. We are intrinsically connected; their pain is my pain.

Most of the world felt incredibly helpless the next

morning when we woke up to new numbers and evidence of the carnage that took place. We mourned collectively, unsure of what to do or how to help. Someone created a blue, white, and red overlay for Facebook profile photos, intended for displaying solidarity with our brothers and sisters in France. It was a way for us to show up and to urge others to show up. One by one I watched my newsfeed fill with faces overlaid by the French flag. It was a loving display of community.

Then an article came out condemning the overlay and those who used it. The article argued that changing a Facebook profile does nothing to actually help the problems of the world, but only helps the individual who did it feel better about themselves while they go about their unchanged lives. I disagree.

I think it connected us for a little while. People in Paris could log on to Facebook and see that the world really did see their pain and care about their trouble. It was a way for us to digitally join hands when we weren't physically able.

When one of us is in trouble, we're all in trouble, and we band together however we can. It's why piles of flowers, five feet deep in some places, were laid outside of Buckingham Palace following the death of Princess Diana. It's why students leave teddy bears and light candles along the fences of schools that have been the target of mass shootings. It's why wreaths are laid on the side of the road at the sites of car accidents.

Maybe these acts don't create any actual physical change in the circumstances of the tragedy, but that isn't the point.

The point is that when trouble comes, we love each other. When trouble comes, we join hands, weep, shout, and show up. Love doesn't have to change the circumstances; love simply needs to enter, stand steady, and offer whatever help it can.

The weight of the world's problems cannot even be carried by the designated helpers. We all have one Helper, the same Helper, and we are called to reflect his light and love and mercy in this world.

Let's not be fair-weather friends. When death or destruction comes to our neighbor's door, let's not change the subject and leave it to the professionals. May we stand up and say, "Stephen's in danger!" as we run to help. Friends love amid the happy and the sad because we are all connected. Because the tallest tree needs the smallest tree. Because we belong to each other.

> LOVE DOESN'T HAVE TO CHANGE THE CIRCUMSTANCES; LOVE SIMPLY NEEDS TO ENTER, STAND STEADY, AND OFFER WHATEVER HELP IT CAN.

twelve

"It's Too Loud My Ears!"

Like most homes with two young children, my house will inevitably get loud and chaotic at points in the day. That is why at least once a day, Mareto cries out, "It's too loud my ears!" When that happens, I can find Mareto with his hands over his ears, his shoulders hunched tight, and a pained look on his face.

I take in our surroundings, and I can see the problem—the TV is playing *Sofia the First*, I have the radio on in the kitchen, Arsema is sitting in a pile of toys and loudly narrating the adventures of her My Little Ponies, and the iPad is explaining step-by-step instructions for how to build a Lego house. Meanwhile the neighbor's dog is barking outside, the dishwasher is humming, and the washing machine is swishing. The microwave just beeped to tell me that my coffee has been reheated for the third time that morning. The UPS delivery truck door just slammed shut, and then the doorbell rang. My phone dinged with a text, and the ice maker just growled as new ice tumbled into the bin.

You and I have learned to tune out all the extra sounds as unimportant background information. Mareto's brain is taking it all in on an equal level. He's processing too much input, and I know that something needs to go. I turn off the TV, move Arsema and her ponies to a different room, turn off the music, and do all I can to simplify his environment. Because Mareto can't tune out, we turn things off.

Maybe we all ought to regularly do the same thing?

It might not be the sounds of the dishwasher, washing machine, microwave, doorbell, or the neighbor's dog that overwhelm our systems. But something else does, because most of us aren't living a completely unplugged life on top of a hill in the middle of nowhere.

We had been married four years when John and I moved to Virginia Beach. We started out our little story in a small town in the mountains of Virginia, but then John decided it was time to attend seminary, so we sold our house, packed our belongings, and moved four hours south. It wasn't earthshaking; I had gone to college nearby, and both sets of parents lived within twenty minutes of our new home. We settled into our new phase and pace of life.

A few months after our move, I made an appointment to see my doctor, certain that I was in serious medical distress. The previous week I'd been experiencing chest pains and heart palpitations practically every morning on my way into work. After an EKG showed that I had not been experiencing heart attacks (as I'd thought), my doctor strapped me to a portable heart monitor just to be safe. As you've probably already guessed, those results were normal as well. I walked away with a prescription for acid reflux medication. It didn't do much.

Over the following weeks and months, I still noticed the occasional tension in my chest and a racing heartbeat. Then John was invited to speak to a group of college students in the town we had moved from the previous year. So we packed a suitcase, pointed our car north, and hit the interstate.

A funny thing happened on that drive out of the city. We passed over the bridge, through the tunnel, past the coliseum, and out of the Hampton Roads area. Soon the road was lined with trees instead of buildings, the interstate narrowed from four lanes to two, the number of cars thinned considerably, and my heart stopped pounding so intensely in my chest.

I took a deep breath and marveled to John about the absolutely undeniable physical and mental transformation that had taken place as we left the city. I had never experienced anything like it before—at least, I didn't remember ever experiencing anything like it. I could actually feel the pressure and discomfort leaving my body.

Here's what felt so surprising and remarkable to me: I didn't even know I was living in a state of discomfort. Seriously. The heart palpitations had gradually become such a normal part of life that I didn't notice them anymore. The tightness in my neck and shoulders from flinching and tensing up had happened so steadily that I wasn't even aware of it.

Or perhaps I wasn't aware anymore because at the first signs of tension or stress or discomfort, I covered it up with something more distracting. I avoided taking the time to listen to what my stress was trying to tell me. I would log into Facebook or Twitter or take Netflix to a new level by binge-watching a new TV show. I turned up the volume on life to drown out the distress rising up inside of me, not realizing that the noise was the very thing causing the problem in the first place.

It wasn't until we left it all in the rearview mirror—the buzzing traffic, the computers with all our emails and messages and tweets and pins, the TV, and even our phones (which we switched to silent mode)—that we had the clarity of mind to realize just how bombarded by chaos our lives had become.

We live in a world of people inwardly screaming, "It's too loud my ears!" But it doesn't work when we try to tune out the noise with more noise, escaping to our earbuds, computers, or phones. Then we wonder why it's so difficult to find the peace and calm we're looking for.

My parents, along with many others, have a great solution to this problem: camping. During one visit with my family, my mom and I struck up a conversation about sleep because she knew how Mareto has a lot of trouble sleeping through the night. (I can count on one hand the number of times Mareto has actually slept from night until morning without getting up at least once.) My mom has trouble sleeping sometimes, too, and she casually mentioned, "You know what always fixes it for me? Camping."

She went on to tell me about studies that had shown how a week of camping essentially hits the reset button in our brains and bodies. It basically restores us to a place of peace and calm and rest.

Well, this piqued my interest, so I went home and looked it up online. I found the studies my mom was talking about and more.[1] The studies about camping led me to studies about our use of smartphones and iPads, which led me to studies about the effects of social media and media in general on our brains.

For instance, the more we use our phones and other devices, the less we're able to focus and not crave the input from those devices. We're vastly cutting short our attention spans. The input from media and social media may be causing a rise in ADHD symptoms in children and adults. We're also becoming desensitized to life. When we live in an alternate reality of television and movies and do all our connecting online, we give ourselves the appearance of a full life, but we can be completely disconnected from reality.

When we allow all the voices of the digital world to overwhelm us, our relationships suffer, our creativity suffers, our bodies and brains suffer, and our spirits cave inside of us. To sum it up, we're getting way too much input, and it's affecting our physical, mental, and spiritual health.

We are far too plugged in and are listening to far too

much noise. Thousands of people shout at us from our TV sets, through our radios, behind our computer screens, in line at Starbucks, in the lane next to us on the highway, and from the phones in our hands.

What do we do?

Well, go camping! Seriously, if that's your thing, then go for it. Pack the sleeping bags, tents, and hiking boots, and head for the woods or desert or valley or mountaintop. Escape for the weekend, or as long as you're able, to unplug, disconnect, and turn down the volume.

But maybe camping isn't really your thing. For some people camping might only amplify the stresses of life. That's okay. You can simplify and learn how to turn off the voices that vie for your attention and energy in your own way and on a daily basis. In fact, I think some daily unplugging is more important than the weekend getaways.

DAILY UNPLUGGING IS MORE IMPORTANT THAN THE WEEKEND GETAWAYS.

John and I couldn't move out of the city and the bustling busyness of that season of life. As much as I wanted to permanently escape to the mountains, it wasn't right or practical for us to leave the city behind. So I started a practice I still use (possibly overuse) today. I made a couple of lists.

First, I listed everything in my life that was taking my

time and attention and speaking into my life and heart—
even subtly so. My list looked (and still looks) something
like this:

- God and my faith journey
- Church and Bible study
- Family and friends
- Husband and children
- Social media: Facebook, Twitter, Pinterest,
  Instagram, blogs
- Work life: emails and phone calls
- Media: TV, movies, radio, magazines, newspapers, books

Then I went back through and made a second list of
everything that was speaking loudest to me and stealing
most of my focus. It was disappointing because I found the
loudest and most persistent voices weren't the life-giving
and peace-bringing voices. I was allowing myself to be
bombarded by social media, obligations and expectations,
television and news, and the constant demands of work and
ministry. It was "too loud my ears!"

All of that noise had come into my life by my own choosing. I had no one to blame but myself; I alone allowed myself
to get sucked into the internet and media vortex. I couldn't
just drive from point A to point B in a calm silence; I had to
crank up the radio and get myself up in arms about some
commentary I disagreed with or some misogynist lyrics getting airtime. I couldn't sit quietly with a cup of tea without

glancing at my phone every few minutes, scrolling my news-feed or Instagram reel, or checking the headlines.

Heavens, we can't even go to the bathroom anymore without bringing our phones with us!

It's like when you were part of a team or a group assignment at school. (What? You didn't love those?) Everyone started talking at once until you finally wanted to scream, but instead the teacher or coach called above the noise, "Stop! One at a time!" That's the adult version of "It's too loud my ears!"

We've essentially invited a bunch of people into our closet with us and allowed them to all start shouting at once. The wonderful thing, the saving grace, is that we can *un-invite* them. The fact that we brought all of this into our lives by choice means that we also have the power to take it out. It's not always easy and it takes conscious effort, but it's so good for our souls.

When Mareto's brain and body have become overloaded, I go into action quickly, turning off everything in the house that is causing his discomfort: the television, radio, dishwasher, everything. I simplify our environment. We quiet and still our little world and sit together in the richness of a pared-down life.

Everyone can do the same thing. Did you know there is a beautiful little "Hide" feature on Facebook? You don't actually have to deactivate your account; you can simply create reasonable boundaries and tune out the loud, angry, offensive, or just plain annoying voices shouting through the screen. You don't have to block your third cousin, but you can make it so that you don't have to see his junk anymore.

We can choose whom we follow on Instagram and Twitter. We can choose to only log into Pinterest to search for a specific recipe or idea, rather than to scroll mindlessly through the two billion projects and wardrobes and home improvement images. We can limit the time we spend watching television. We can delete the apps on our phone and turn off the notifications that ping us.

When I think of simplicity, of peace, of solitude, my mind rushes to Psalm 42. The first verse in particular paints a picture that encapsulates quiet refreshment: "As a deer pants for flowing streams, so pants my soul for you, O God." In my mind I see a fawn at dusk, leaning into the fresh, clear water, birds slowing their songs, the last rays of sun stretching pink and orange across the sky, and deep, quiet refreshment.

I love this passage of scripture so much because it is the cry of a tired man's heart. A man who is being shouted at and oppressed and taunted by the soul-sucking voices in his life. A man who just longs for a moment of peace and refreshment and quiet. Does that feel familiar?

We likely aren't being hunted by a physical enemy the way he was, but we are being taunted by a spiritual enemy who uses any means he can to cause unrest and chaos in our lives. For some reason—maybe it's as simple as not being aware of our own stress—we fail to create healthy boundaries and silence the unhealthy voices in our lives.

Like Mareto, we need to start tuning out the noise—unplugging, logging out, and breathing in the simplicity of life lived with the people who mean the most to us. Because if we're not careful, we'll miss the most important messages of life by unintentionally drowning them out.

thirteen

"LOOK AROUND—I NEED TO TALK FOR YOU!"

Mareto knows when I'm not listening well. For a variety of reasons, there are times when I'm not exactly paying attention to him. Maybe he's been telling me a story I'm struggling to follow while I fold laundry. Maybe I'm answering emails while he's asking a question. Whatever the reason for my halfhearted listening, Mareto notices, and he doesn't like it.

Soon two little hands frame my face as he turns my face into his. Then he makes direct eye contact and blurts out a frustrated, "Mommy! Look around! I need to talk for you!"

Something about Mareto's reaction to my distraction struck me one day. I thought about what he was doing and what he was asking of me. Of course what he means is, "Stop what you are doing, turn toward me, and listen to what I am saying to you!" In other words, Mareto wants me to listen to him with my whole body.

Have you ever been talking to someone who seemed to be not all that into you or your conversation? They aren't making eye contact, and their face is tilted slightly away. They don't offer up the little interjections of "mmhmm" and "yes" or "really?" or "right!" as you're talking. Not even the polite head nod to show they are following along. You know they're not really listening because of their body language.

Listening is a full-body exercise. (That is why, side note, it's not a great idea to talk on the phone while you're driving.) We've become a society of bad listeners.

Perhaps it's all those voices we have in our lives that make us terrible listeners. We're so used to all the noise that we have a hard time stopping to focus and listen well to the voices that matter. We miss out on a lot of good input—input from God, from our loved ones, from voices with wisdom in them. We'll miss the invaluable treasure if we don't stop long enough to hear the message.

Mareto has been an incredible example to me of what it means to listen with your whole body. Eye contact can be hard for him, especially when it's demanded

WE'LL MISS THE INVALUABLE TREASURE IF WE DON'T STOP LONG ENOUGH TO HEAR THE MESSAGE.

and not a spontaneous choice he's made. When I have very important instructions for him, or something special to tell him, he looks off to the side or over my shoulder. He's not being rude. He's listening.

I'm so thankful that a speech therapist explained this lack of eye contact during conversation early on in Mareto's life. She told us that demanding eye contact from him was actually making it harder for Mareto to listen, because it was requiring an unusual amount of focus and thought to simply look us in the eye. She encouraged us to let him gaze off into the distance and see what happened.

She was absolutely right. What happened was Mareto could understand and process our instructions or conversation remarkably faster when we let him be instead of asking him to look at us. Mareto knew what he was doing all along when he instinctively stared over my shoulder while I spoke. He was removing all distraction so that he could listen well.

Most of us don't have a problem with listening while making eye contact, but we do have other things that steal our focus, take up our energy, and prevent us from truly listening to the voices of the ones who matter most. Worries about the day follow us home, or work consumes our thoughts at the dinner table. And then we realize we haven't heard a word of the story our child was sharing about her school day. Work, school, friends, family issues, church issues, politics, to-do lists, money problems, chores, health issues, and more consume our thoughts and distract us away from the people we love.

Even things that are meant to connect us and help us listen to one another are driving us apart. Consider social media, email, and phones. When used in a healthy way, they promote relationships—but only if we use them as tools for listening and connecting more than we use them for amplifying our own agenda.

I saw a pie chart on Facebook recently meant to be both humorous and educational. The entire circle was red, and off to the side was the key to the chart. Blue stood for the percentage of people who changed their views (on politics, religion, or anything at all) based on other people's Facebook statuses. Red represented the percentage of people who didn't change their views at all. The point, of course, was that no one changes their mind based on what they read on Facebook. There's no way to know if that's entirely true, but it makes a good point.

So often we log on to social media or attend book clubs and Bible studies or sit in mom groups and in coffee shops to share our own thoughts and opinions. We like to hear our own voices far more than we admit, and we struggle to listen well to the person sitting next to us on the couch or across from us at the table.

How often have you been in the following situation: You're engaged in what you feel is a meaningful discussion with someone you value when suddenly your conversation is interrupted by a loud *buzz* and *ding*. You glance at your phone but, deciding it would be rude, you choose not to check the text message you've just received. You encourage your friend to continue, but a couple minutes later the *buzz* and *ding* happens again. Then a few more times. You apologize, check your messages, type off a quick response, and look back up to your friend.

You encourage her, saying, "So sorry! Go on . . ." But she says she forgot what she was saying and asks how you've been. Maybe she did forget, or maybe she didn't feel like you were really listening. I've been guilty of that very scenario too many times.

The other evening, I stood in the kitchen sharing something about my day with my husband. We usually leave our laptop to charge in a little corner where the counter meets the refrigerator, and it's often left open. John's email browser was up, and as I was talking he noticed a few new emails coming in. He turned to open the emails while simultaneously telling me, "Keep talking. I'm listening!"

I tried for a minute but then got discouraged and decided to wait.

All of a sudden he shook his head and closed the computer. "What am I doing? I'm sorry. I can check those at work in the morning. Go ahead. I'm really listening now."

It meant a lot that he quickly recognized that half-hearted listening wasn't actual listening, and that important relationships deserve our full attention.

That's something I have tried to be more aware of on my own. A couple of years ago I made a choice to stop rushing through bedtime with my children. It happened sort of by accident. I was going through the typical bedtime routine with Arsema—reading a few books, singing a few songs, then tucking her into bed—and something precious happened. I leaned over to give her one last kiss, and she started talking.

She told me about all the things she did that day. I heard stories from school, and I learned what stood out to her as special at home. She asked me questions and told me what she wanted to do the next day. I heard her say things like, "Maybe we'll go to a basketball game?" and, "Will you paint my toesies in the morning?"

But I almost missed out on it. In my exhaustion and preoccupation with my to-do list, I've cut her off early in the course of too many other evenings. When she first started to talk to me at bedtime, I listened for a moment before telling her that it was time for bed and that we'd talk in the morning. But when morning came she had either forgotten what she was going to share with me, or she simply didn't want to anymore. I felt a twinge of disappointment and then went on with the day. After a few mornings like this, I decided to let her talk at night—and the result was meaningful connection.

Now this beautiful scene plays out at the end of each day by her bedside: I learn what is important to my daughter. As she shares her memories and things she misses or looks forward to, I get a glimpse of her heart. We get uninterrupted time to connect as the room is quiet and still and dark. She isn't competing with anything or anyone else for my attention. Arsema and I are together, and she blossoms. I have learned to be still and quiet and to talk only if she asks me a question or if I need to let her know I'm listening. I don't guide her words or try to teach her things as I sometimes do during the day. This time is my turn to sit and learn from her.

When it's my turn to put Mareto to bed, he does something similar. Usually he shares one or two things about his day or something hilarious from his imagination and then falls asleep. These moments are treasures.

THERE IS SOMETHING SO SWEET ABOUT THE STILL AND QUIET SILENCE THAT FOSTERS OPEN-HEART SHARING.

I've learned that there is something so sweet about the still and quiet silence that fosters open-heart sharing. I've learned that there is no to-do list more important than listening to my children, and that they are sharing the most profound bits of their hearts in the whispers of evening.

It reminds me of the story of God visiting Elijah in 1 Kings. Elijah had just killed the false prophets of Baal and was now fleeing a furious Jezebel, who threatened to kill him in retaliation. He found a cave and hid there until the voice of the Lord told him to go stand on a mountain. And this is the part I love so much:

The Lord said, "Go out and stand on the mountain in the presence of the Lord, for the Lord is about to pass by."
Then a great and powerful wind tore the mountains

apart and shattered the rocks before the LORD, but the LORD was not in the wind. After the wind there was an earthquake, but the LORD was not in the earthquake. After the earthquake came a fire, but the LORD was not in the fire. And after the fire came a gentle whisper. (1 Kings 19:11–12 NIV)

As you might have already guessed, the Lord was in the whisper. And as Elijah listened to the whisper, the Lord told him what to do.

Other versions of Scripture refer to this as a "still small voice," which has become a popular phrase to use in faith circles today. When we are wondering about the path our life should take, when things are hard and we feel uncertain, we are encouraged to listen to that "still small voice." But we can't hear it if we're paying attention to the wind and the earthquake and the fire.

Being distracted makes it incredibly difficult, if not impossible, to listen to the voice of God. I've never heard God speaking to me in an audible voice (gentle whisper or other-wise), but there have been plenty of occasions when I could tell God was using little moments to speak to me. But they are often small and quiet and easy to miss if I'm not paying attention.

I've already told you about the Friday in June when I first read about a baby girl in Ethiopia who was waiting for a fam-ily. When I first showed John her pictures and information, I have to admit I was initially discouraged when he said we needed the weekend to pray over such a big decision. I wanted to call the adoption agency immediately and tell them we were ready to sign any and all paperwork to get the ball rolling.

Then Saturday came and went with no clear answer from John. If I'm being honest, I wasn't really praying much about it with him. I had made up my mind on my own and didn't believe I needed any additional confirmation. But John takes his time with decisions and thinks through everything. He was patient and listened to my reasons for why this was the right thing for our family. But he wanted more than anything to hear from God.

One of the agreements we made with each other that Friday was that we wouldn't tell a single soul we were considering adopting Arsema. No one knew about the Facebook post I'd seen. In fact, the only thing anyone knew about our adoption plans was that the Ghana program we'd been looking into seemed to be closing, so we were waiting to see what would happen. John and I both kept our word and kept this decision between us and God.

On Sunday morning I stood in my husband's small office at the church where he was working. It was the bustling fifteen minutes between Sunday school and the service, and he was shuffling through papers and organizing attendance sheets and lessons while I tried to keep Mareto out of the desk drawers. A little girl we didn't know well at all walked in with a rumpled brown paper sack. She said she had something for us, and I smiled at her when John glanced up from the desk, still somewhat distracted.

She pulled a little doll with long yellow yarn for hair out of her sack and handed it to me. "This is for you, because she looks like you," she said with a shy smile. I thanked her and smiled and went to give her a hug, but then she reached her hand back into the sack. She pulled out a second doll. This one had black curly yarn for hair, and her skin was made out of brown fabric. "This one is for your little girl." She handed me the doll, spun around, and left. I looked up to see John's shocked face mirroring my own emotions. He quickly shut the door to his office, and I couldn't stop the amazed tears that had begun spilling over my cheeks.

We hugged for a moment, then John looked down at me and said, "Well, clearly she's ours! We can call the agency after church."

It wasn't an audible voice that told us Arsema was our daughter, but do I believe God spoke to us through the actions of a little girl who had no idea what was going on in our lives? Absolutely. God had spoken and we, thank goodness, were listening. I had only been in a position to really listen, because my husband had told me that's what we needed to do. I'm so grateful for it, because a few months later when Mareto was diagnosed with autism and I was feeling afraid and worried about the changes our family was facing, I could go back to that moment after Sunday school and know that this was right.

Some of the best decisions and the sweetest bits of insight and wisdom come from listening. Truly listening builds relationships, because we open our ears and hearts to another's thoughts, dreams, hopes, fears, and worldview. Society may be training us to talk over each other and shout to be heard, but I think there's hope for change if we can quiet ourselves and follow Mareto's instructions to listen with our whole bodies.

fourteen

"I CAN. I WILL. I BELIEVE."

Mareto struggles with fear on a daily basis. Many of his fears are related to not knowing what to expect. What a familiar feeling that is! If only we could glimpse into the future . . . but then again, maybe it's best that we can't.

Mareto struggles with fear of food in particular. This is a tough one for John and me to understand because we love to eat. Mareto's diet consists of about three foods, and we've tried over and over to introduce new things into his repertoire. He even refuses most sweets, which I know he'd love if he'd just try them.

One day his therapist explained it to us in terms that we could understand. She said, "Imagine it's a hot summer day, and you've poured yourself a drink. You take a big gulp, expecting ice-cold Coke. But when the liquid hits your mouth, you realize it's room-temperature milk. That's what it's like for Mareto every single time he tries an unfamiliar food."

Well, yikes. I'd be afraid to try new things too!

These days Mareto faces his fears by reciting a phrase he learned at school: "I can. I will. I believe." It hasn't worked with food yet, but in most other areas he is learning to step beyond his comfort zone. His little phrase is like an internal pep talk—muttering to his brain and heart, "I can do this! I can do this!"

I am afraid of many things as well: airplanes, public speaking, the future, losing a loved one. Our fears can often cloud reality and tell us a different story than what is actually true. Sometimes, though, our fears are actually quite justified.

OUR FEARS CAN OFTEN CLOUD REALITY AND TELL US A DIFFERENT STORY THAN WHAT IS ACTUALLY TRUE.

My battle with fear isn't new; it began in childhood. My earliest memories of fear are meshed with *all* of my earliest memories. Back then I slept with a night-light to help my fear of the dark. Many nights, though, I would still wake from a nightmare with a pounding heart. When I couldn't go back to sleep, I'd wander down the hall to my parents' room.

As I grew, so did my fears. Maybe I was afraid to try out for the basketball team, or to play my violin in the recital, or to ride the roller coasters at Knot's Berry Farm—basic, fairly regular childhood fears. Then there were, of course, the not-so-normal fears: of my house burning down like the one down the street, or the ice rink blowing up like the federal building in Oklahoma City. But I learned to bury those fears deep down and leave them unaddressed.

To help me combat my fear and nerves, my dad gave me a helpful tool and told me to ask myself, "What's the worst that could happen?" His method did actually help as I weathered childhood and adolescence.

For me, in my fairly sheltered and privileged middle-class American life, the worst that could happen were feelings of disappointment after not making the team, or not getting to play in the chamber symphony after screwing up an audition. When I forgot a few notes of my piece in the recital, I flailed around until I got back on track. Yes, I was a little embarrassed, but it wasn't the end of the world. I'd forgotten about it by the end of the week.

Maybe a boy I liked wouldn't like me back—and in junior high that really does feel like the end of the world—so I'd crank up my Alanis Morrisette tape in my room and lament my heartache . . . until the next month, when I had a crush on a new boy.

"The worst that could happen" in those growing-up years wasn't ever that bad. Not making the basketball team in ninth grade was a huge disappointment, especially because I had strep throat during tryouts and was running ragged. But I worked hard and made the team the following year.

When it came time to apply for college, the worst that could happen was that I wouldn't be accepted into the school that I really wanted to attend. And guess what? That's exactly what happened. I chose another school, hated it, transferred to yet another school during my sophomore year, and met my husband a few months later.

Every time I let my thoughts ride to the end of "the worst that could happen" and it *actually* happened, I found out that "the worst" wasn't really that bad.

Then one day, the worst that could happen really *was* that bad, and my little tool to combat my fears utterly failed me. The hypothetical question just didn't help much anymore, because when I got pregnant, "the worst that could happen" was to lose my baby. And I did.

After I had my first miscarriage, the careful walls I'd erected to lock up any really serious fears came tumbling down. The foundations were completely destroyed. Fear flooded my heart and rose to the surface, and I didn't think there was anything I could do about it.

So I lived with it. I let my anxiety fester until it started making a difference in my daily life. I became somewhat of a hermit and explained it away to my husband by saying I loved our cozy home and liked to spend time inside. I went camping exactly three times, because each time we climbed in the tent or walked into the woods I came up with a thousand reasons for why we would perish there.

When I became a mom, I worried about sending my children to school, not because I was like any other mom (reluctant to let go), but because I was terrified of losing the ability to protect them from predators or mass shootings or natural disasters. Even the playground and the backyard became scary for me as my children grew and stretched their minds, bodies, and limits by taking risks and trying new things.

Eventually I found myself up in the middle of the night, trying to crawl out of my skin and panting for breath. Then it would hit in the middle of the day—nausea, shortness of breath, and the need to run away from what terrified me. Except my fear was on the inside, and there was no escape.

Panic attacks, I was told.

I landed on a deep couch with huge cushions, across from a counselor with compassionate eyes and a warm smile. As I shared my memories and thoughts and fears with her, she asked me what I felt.

"Afraid. And tired."

"Yes, but what else? What are you believing that is making you so afraid?"

"I don't know. I guess that I need to be in control."

"Yes and?"

"I don't know..." The tears started to fall. I was so tired. "I guess I just worry that if I don't make the exact right choice at the exact right minute that something awful is going to happen to the people I love."

That was it right there. The fear of the unknown and the fear of not being in control of what happens to me and the people I love.

We sat while my tears fell, and she asked me to seek out the truth. "You're believing a lie, Lauren," she said. "Somewhere deep in there you aren't believing the truth about something. You might know the truth in your head, but you aren't really living by it. What is the truth to that statement you just made, that it's all up to you? That if you don't make the right choice something bad is going to happen to you and the people you love?"

I sat in the quiet and closed my eyes. Soon I began praying, pleading in my heart with God to help me figure this out. Truth came rushing in.

"God is sovereign," I whispered. "I know that he has good plans for me, not to hurt me but to help me."

I knew in my head that God was in control and that he was good, but my poor heart just couldn't quite believe it.

In the same way, Mareto knows we love him. I mean, I tell him about four hundred times a day in between hugs and snuggles and play. So when I offer him a blueberry muffin, I want him to know that I'm giving him something good. Something he'll enjoy. I tell him it's yummy and ask him to just try it. He looks at me, and I can see the anxiety in his eyes. He wants to believe me, but he doesn't quite yet.

Aren't we all works in progress that way?

I love the image of God that C. S. Lewis paints in his novel *The Lion, the Witch, and the Wardrobe*. The children, who have found themselves in this magical kingdom after wandering through an old door in the back of the closet, are asking a couple of beavers about Aslan—the lion who reminds us of God. They first wonder if he is a man, but when they hear he is a lion, they grow nervous about meeting him. Lucy asks if he is safe, and Mr. Beaver responds: "Safe? . . . Don't you hear what Mrs. Beaver tells you? Who said anything about safe? 'Course he isn't safe. But he's good. He's the King, I tell you."[1]

That may be the problem for most of us. We want a reassurance of safety. We want to know that the worst that can happen really isn't all that bad, and when it is, we stop trusting in the goodness of God. We can't even focus on it anymore, because all we see is that he is not safe. And we begin to believe that it's up to us to make sure bad things don't happen in our little corner of the world.

That, of course, is a lie and completely impossible. Combating fear must start here. We have to dig into the lie and uncover the truth waiting below.

Mareto's little phrase, "I can. I will. I believe," is a great starting point. He's learned that speaking the truth about a situation is the first step in facing fear. Truth helps us to be brave, even in our fear.

I've struggled with 1 John 4:18, which says, "There is no fear in love, but perfect love casts out fear," mainly because it's difficult for me to imagine life without fear. I believe in love and its power, so I have wondered if I just need more faith or more love to get rid of my anxiety.

TRUTH HELPS US TO BE BRAVE, EVEN IN OUR FEAR.

But life has shown me what I believe that verse really means.

As I have mentioned, flying is a fear of mine. I absolutely hate the helpless feeling that overcomes me when I board a plane. I'm a sweaty, trembling mess. On one particularly bumpy flight, an attendant actually knelt beside me to ask if I was going to be okay because I was nearly hyperventilating and the skin on my chest and neck had turned into a bright red splotchy disaster. This fear of mine isn't a small annoyance; it's a full-blown phobia.

I had arranged my life as an adult so that I wouldn't have to fly. All my relatives were within reasonable driving distance, and I didn't care to vacation overseas at the cost of boarding a plane. It had been nearly a decade since I had last been on an airplane when John and I finally decided to adopt.

We had done all the research, we had looked into domestic adoption, and we had been foster parents; but at the end of the day none of it felt like the right path. But a program in Ethiopia kept coming up, and the more we looked into it, the more peace we felt about going in that direction. I don't know why we felt that way, except that it's just where we were supposed to go. So we turned in our application and started our adoption process with excitement and dedication.

I knew, of course, that we would eventually have to fly to Ethiopia to bring home our child, but I tucked that away behind a locked door in the corner of my mind. Then, when we were a few months into our wait to be matched, we got a call from our adoption agency. Ethiopia had made a new law that would now require adopting parents to travel to Ethiopia twice before bringing their child home. I nearly flipped out.

Now, hear me: This law is good. It is extremely hard on parents and children alike, but it is a necessary step in combating fraud, trafficking, and unlawful practices. This step allows the Ethiopian government and the United States government time to investigate each case and for the parents to actually meet their child and go to court in person to claim them as their own.

I was flipping out solely because this meant I would have to fly around the world twice, when once was already more than my brain could handle. I didn't even care about the added expense this would bring; I was simply freaking out about those flights.

The day finally came for our first flight out of Washington DC. I was in tears by the time the plane began to speed down the runway for its ascent into the sky (and our eventual death, I was convinced). But I did it. Why? Because I love Mareto.

I think that verse in 1 John is saying that when we truly love, when we have perfect love in our hearts, fear has no power over us anymore. Fear cannot stop us from acting out of a place of genuine love.

I was still a ball of jumpy nerves on my flights to and from Ethiopia. I didn't sleep (which made jet lag extra fun), and I could barely choke down my food. But fear did not have the power to stop me from going to get my son. I love him so fully and completely and wholly that I would fly across oceans for him (which, to me, is the equivalent of walking through fire).

I knew that God had led us to Ethiopia, and my love for my son was and is unbreakable. I wish I'd had Mareto's little phrase during those flights. I would have whispered to myself, "I can. I will. I believe."

Our God is not safe. He calls us out to hard and scary things. Faith in him requires levels of trust that seem nearly impossible, but we stand in the power of God's love and face our fears with the truth of his goodness and sovereignty. We can believe the truth in the face of our fears, and we need to remember that we *can* do hard things, that we *will* do hard things, and that we believe in Someone who is bigger than our fear.

We can.

We will.

We believe.[2]

fifteen

"Or Yes, or No?"

It's Saturday morning, and we're all moving slowly. John is prepping a sermon at the kitchen table, and I'm sipping hot coffee in the corner chair in the living room while our pajama-clad children sprawl out on the carpet with their blankets and toys. I watch them play some made-up game and enjoy the relative peace and calm. Then Mareto pops his head up and turns to me. "Where are we going today?"

I tell him I don't know, that we don't have any plans yet, but he doesn't accept that answer. A little more adamantly he asks, "Or school or church?" I explain that it's Saturday, and that means no school and no church. It's the one day of the week that isn't preplanned, the one morning of the week without a schedule and a place to go.

Saturdays can be tough on Mareto. He prefers simplicity. He sees black and white in an increasingly gray world. He wants things to be clear and the path, the choice, to be obvious. He prefers a "yes or no" world with clear answers, and he doesn't respond well to answers like "not yet" or "maybe later" or "I don't know" or "we'll see." The vagueness confuses and overwhelms him.

A few weeks ago Mareto had a checkup with his pediatrician. She had warned us at a previous appointment that Mareto would need vaccinations the next time he came in. Every single time we take Mareto to the doctor, he asks if he is going to get a shot. Usually we can reassure him with an empathic, "No shots today!" This day was, of course, different.

About halfway through the checkup Mareto looked at John and asked, "Am I going to get a shot?"

John responded with Mareto's least favorite answer: "Not right now, Mareto."

Mareto continued to ask multiple times, getting the same response from John. Finally, he got exasperated and blurted out, "Or yes, or no, Daddy?!"

I see a lot of myself in Mareto. In fact, I see Mareto in all of us. He boils down just about every decision to a choice between two things. Holding up his Transformers toys before church, he cocks his head to the side and says, "Or yes or no?" He wants to take them to Sunday school and needs an answer. Waking up on a Tuesday he looks up from his place at the breakfast table and asks, "Or school or church?" Ice cream is either chocolate or vanilla, and shoes are either sneakers or sandals. Life is easier that way, and manageable. Aren't we all craving simplicity?

In his book *The Paradox of Choice: Why More Is Less*, Barry Schwartz said, "According to a survey conducted by Yankelovich Partners, a majority of people want more control over the details of their lives, but a majority of people also want to simplify their lives. There you have it—the paradox of our times."[1]

Indeed. Most of us desperately want to simplify our lives. We want things to be as easy as "yes or no," but we find ourselves labored with endless decisions day after day. Instead of a clear-cut choice between two or three options, we find that there are several options for every choice we have to make.

Should we homeschool or private school or public school or unschool or do Montessori? Should we follow a paleo diet, a vegan diet, or the Atkins diet? What type of treatment or therapy should we try—ABA, GFCF diet, Western medications, or a mix? Should we choose a denomination or go with the nondenominational church? And if we choose a denomination, which one? We do a quick Google search and find thirty-six churches of the same denomination in our city. Maybe we should do a home church?

As consumers we're offered endless possibilities for almost any product we could want to purchase. Between the various brands and versions and service providers and upgrades and models, buying a phone becomes the source of weeks and weeks of research. As much as I love my smartphone, I kind of miss the days of leaning against the kitchen wall with the mile-long cord twisted around my body.

It's even difficult to decide what to eat for dinner! Some

evenings my husband offers to pick up takeout for us to enjoy after the kids go to bed. With the best intentions he asks, "What do you want to eat?" and I'm immediately over-whelmed and stressed out.

"Can you just throw out a couple options, and I'll tell you if there's anything I don't want?" I beg. I just don't feel like I have decision-making capabilities by the end of the day.

Schwartz explains in his book that learning to choose well is hard, but that it's even harder for us (perhaps too hard) because we live in a world of endless possibilities. When we're given the choice between chocolate ice cream and vanilla, most of us can decide quickly. But take me to the local gelato place, and I'll stand in front of the glass looking at the dozens of buckets of gelato and take fifteen minutes to make my choice. It's overwhelming.

My husband has been ministering to middle school students through college-aged young adults for a decade. We love the young men and women we've served, but I am incredibly grateful to be in my thirties and out of that mas-sive transitional season of life. Young people are plagued with indecision that leaves them feeling paralyzed and second-guessing themselves at every turn. I've met with young women who overanalyze every little choice in life to death, some huge decisions and some so inconsequential that I can't understand their level of stress over it. I think it comes from having so many choices to make at a young age—choices that supposedly will impact the rest of their lives.

Going to college isn't good enough anymore. Now they must choose between lists of schools, and they must choose the best one. Once they've chosen a college, it's time to select a major, and the list to choose from is as long or longer than the list of schools they applied to. Then they have work and internships and friendships and clubs and romantic relationships and trips abroad or sports camps. With every choice comes endless options, and it's overwhelming.

A phrase I heard often as a young adult in response to certain decisions I faced was, "If you do (insert choice A here), it will be the biggest mistake of your life." Have you noticed yet that we're a culture of exaggeration? I love Ellen DeGeneres's take on this in one of her standup acts from years ago.[2] She takes on the phrase "Oh, that's the worst!" and how people use it to describe paper cuts.

"Really? That's the worst? What about pickle juice in your eye? That's pretty bad too!" The point is, we overdramatize and overthink every little detail of our lives. We're obsessed with the extremes . . . the worst or the biggest mistake and the best possible choice.

Schwartz calls people who seek out the absolute best in every possible situation the "maximizers." These people research for weeks and months before buying a product to be sure they got the absolute best. They agonize over decisions because they're worried a better option is out there. But there is another way.

"The alternative to maximizing," he argues, "is to be a

satisficer. To satisfice is to settle for something that is good enough and not worry about the possibility that there might be something better."[3]

He goes on to say that we should simply focus on what matters most to us in life—those things that are meaningful and important to who we are and how we live. We don't have to live constantly searching for the best thing out there; we can look at what brings us joy and life and focus on good enough.

Good enough might actually be God's best for us. God's best for the mom down the street might not be the best for me. Our culture's growing obsession with being or having the biggest and the best has led to dissatisfaction and an overabundance of options. We waste time worrying that something better is out there, unknown to us.

And while too many choices leave us feeling stuck and overwhelmed, having no choice can be equally as paralyzing.

When we moved from the beach to the mountains, the kids were quite small. Mareto had recently turned three, and Arsema was about eighteen months

> WE DON'T HAVE TO LIVE CONSTANTLY SEARCHING FOR THE BEST THING OUT THERE; WE CAN LOOK AT WHAT BRINGS US JOY AND LIFE AND FOCUS ON GOOD ENOUGH.

old. My husband left a fairly standard church job (Sunday school and adult service with nursery and children's church available) for a chaplain's position at a military college. For the first year I juggled the children in the foyer of the chapel every Sunday morning. They were too young to sit quietly in the service, and there were no childcare options.

It was a long, hard year, and it ended with me feeling like the spiritual, mental, and emotional equivalent of a prune. I was dried up and withering. I stayed home with the children all day every day, then sat in the foyer on Sunday mornings while everyone else worshipped together. I hadn't really formed close friendships or deep community, and I felt worn out and raw. I tried hard for a year to make it work (even though it clearly didn't work at all) because I thought I had no choice. This was my husband's new job and new ministry; there were no other options.

By the end of that first year I had reached my limit. John and I talked the topic inside out trying to figure out what the possibilities were until we finally reached a decision: the children and I would find a church that was family (kid) friendly, even though we hated to separate our family on Sunday mornings. The best option would be for us to be together, but the best wasn't possible—so we settled for good enough. It wasn't fair to me or the kids to have to sit in a foyer for two hours every Sunday morning, so we decided to find someplace else.

Our search for a church narrowed down to a handful of local churches, and I knew that the staff would need to be open to accommodating Mareto's autism. You'd think that would be a no-brainer, that every church would respond with open arms, but that was sadly not the case. I've actually found that to find church staff and church family ready to embrace a special-needs family and figure out how to meet the needs of the children is kind of rare and incredible. I sent emails to the head pastors of each church on my list, explaining our unique situation and our unique family. A couple never responded, a couple responded that they couldn't meet the needs of my son in Sunday school or children's church, and one responded that he would be happy to meet our family any morning that week.

Of course, that's the church we visited, and during our meeting with the pastor, I said that I was looking around at all my options. I hoped he would not be offended if I attended one Sunday but not the next. (I was "church shopping," as some folks call it.) He was gracious and understanding, then gave me the number for the children's ministry director. By the end of the week, everything was in place for me and the kids to attend church that Sunday.

Our first visit was great. The kids loved their class, and the staff was welcoming and understanding of Mareto. I sat uninterrupted through both adult Sunday school and the service with a hot cup of coffee. For the first time in a year, I got to worship God alongside other people without a heavy wooden door and glass windows separating us. I left feeling loved and refreshed, and honestly I tried not to cry through most of the service as I was so overcome with relief.

You know what? I never visited another church. I had planned to "church shop," but I never did. I couldn't quite muster the energy or see the point. I had found a church that I enjoyed and that loved and accepted my family.

Is there a better church out there somewhere? Possibly. Does it matter? No. Because where we are is good enough. It's better than good enough, because I believe it's God's best for us right now.

Proverbs 3:5–6 says, "Trust in the LORD with all your heart, and do not lean on your own understanding. In all your ways acknowledge him, and he will make straight your paths." This is such a well-known and oft-quoted verse, and there's a reason for that. In it we find the comforting reassurance that God will make our paths known, that what we need is to trust him. It's a reminder not to worry or overthink every detail of life.

Verse five starts with the word *trust*. Instead of fretting over every little decision and option we are presented with, we can trust that God is in the details of life. We don't actually need to micromanage our lives to pieces. God won't let us walk down an eternally destructive path, sighing, "Oh well . . . she made the wrong choice. She had a million options, and she picked the wrong one." God's not out to get us, and life isn't supposed to be a puzzle set on the hardest level.

I hear God in those verses saying to his people, "Hey, trust me. Really trust that I have your best interests at heart. Don't overanalyze every little thing that comes your way, and don't overthink every step. Just seek me, love me, and follow me. And I'll steer you in the right direction."

Mareto started preschool just after turning four. We found a small special-education class with peer buddies and an amazing teacher. I was nervous, but Mareto loved it. Over the course of the year, we saw Mareto make progress and gain confidence, so much so that the teachers and staff at his school thought he was ready to start kindergarten the following year. I had a feeling in my gut that this wasn't the right choice, but the options and information presented to us at the meeting seemed to fit with their recommendation. We signed off on it, and at the end of August Mareto started kindergarten.

From August to December Mareto cried every morning before we dropped him off and every day after we picked him up from school. Week after week he became more emotionally fragile and withdrawn. We had numerous meetings with his teachers and the school staff to try to fix the problem. His joy was fading, and I lay awake night after night worrying about my son. Finally, over Christmas break, we made the choice to pull Mareto out of school. I had agonized for over a month about this decision. I'd looked at every option and thought about every recommendation, but in the end it was really quite simple. My son was miserable, and he didn't need to be.

After Christmas break Mareto went to a new preschool (a typical class that fell nicely between the special-ed preschool and the kindergarten class), and he loved it. His excitement about learning and friends returned, and he never cried on the way to school. In the mornings he talked about what he was going to learn or show his friends and teachers. Our little boy—full of joy and life—was back.

The choice was so easy in the end because I narrowed it down to "or yes or no." Did it matter if Mareto could read and write at five instead of six years old? No. Did it matter that he was miserable every single day? Yes. It really was an easy decision when I let the peripherals go—my worries about the other options and the opinions of the other teachers and staff—when I looked at our family priorities, and when I listened to my mother's intuition. I followed Mareto's lead and brought it back to "or yes or no."

Every choice facing us might not be "or yes or no," but we can always cut out the excess and bring things back down to the simplest possible answers when we feel overwhelmed. Whether it's church or school or jobs or even deciding what to cook for dinner, we can avoid decision-fatigue by streamlining whenever possible.

Mareto reminds us of the value of paring down—of looking at what's important, of examining our priorities, and of simplifying our choices. When I live like that I find more peace and joy, and fewer restless nights.

sixteen

"This Is My Mommy"

When Mareto started school we made the transition carefully. Every morning I'd park the car, walk him to the classroom, and wait a couple minutes until he seemed well adjusted before leaving to go about our morning. And every single morning for those first few months Mareto entered the classroom the same way: he would enthusiastically introduce himself and me to the entire class.

"It's me, Nato! This is my mommy!"

His teachers would laugh and join him in his excitement. "We know you! Come on in!" With a pleased smile he'd settle in to play next to his peers. We'd laugh with the teachers too, but as we drove away from the school I always had a little lump in my throat.

My little boy knows me. He knows my name, and he wants to share that with the world. Mareto knows us, and he is proud of us, as shown by his constant desire to introduce his family to everyone he sees—no matter how many times we've met them before.

We all want to be known. We want to be known for who we really are—all the many facets of our personalities and roles in life. We are multidimensional beings, and there is something special about each position we hold and the recognition of those positions by the people in our lives. I am a wife, daughter, sister, friend, niece, cousin, aunt, and granddaughter. I am also a writer, occasional speaker, and ministry leader. I am a Christian. I've been a Sunday school teacher and babysitter and administrative assistant. And I am a mother.

My roles, past and present, have played an important part in who I am today, and they constitute a part of the mosaic of my personality and spirit and passion. I've been a basketball player and a violinist. I've been on the debate team and part of the model UN. I've loved ballet and swimming and gymnastics. I've been a beach bum and a hiker. But of all the roles I've held in my life, the relational roles are by far the most important to me.

I was born into many of those positions. I entered the world as a daughter to two loving and happily married parents, as a sister to a big sister waiting at home for me, and a granddaughter to two sets of grandparents hoping to spoil me rotten. I had aunts and uncles, a growing list of cousins to play with during holidays, and eventually, a younger brother. Then I made friends, some for a short time and whose names and faces I don't remember. Others have made a lasting imprint on my heart and my life.

I was kindergarten-age when I made my first best friends. We moved from Monterey, California, down to San Diego and soon met the neighbors. Two boys, with whom we shared a backyard fence, bounded into our home one day while our moms got to know each other. They were the exact ages of my sister and me, and it was clear we would be buddies. Nick and my sister were older and therefore cooler, but Ryan and I had our own fun.

Ryan always wanted to do things that involved me stubbing my toes or tearing the skin off my knees, but I didn't care because he was my friend. He pushed me to do things like biking over jumps and rollerblading down steep hills without brakes. We fought like siblings, and Ryan taught me that you can be friends with someone and still get mad at them from time to time.

At school Ryan was part of the popular group (it still amazes me that kids that young even care about those things), and I was most certainly not. We didn't hang out at school much, but I always knew we were friends because we really knew each other. On the streets in our neighborhood and in the backyard, it didn't matter what cliques we were in.

The year I started kindergarten I met a girl named Katie. My mom found out that Katie lived about two blocks away, and one afternoon we walked down to her house together to invite Katie over to play. From then on we were inseparable. Katie and I had different personalities and interests. She had two older brothers and an older sister and loved the Tasmanian Devil from Looney Tunes. She wore oversized T-shirts and sometimes said bad words, while I was into Barbies and makeup and ballet. I didn't know any bad words (until Katie taught me). For some reason we were perfectly, oppositely compatible, and we told each other absolutely everything. Katie taught me that it's amazingly wonderful to have friends who know you inside out and that it's a special gift to have friends who are different from you.

Ryan and Katie made me not care about being part of the popular crowd, because they knew me and loved me—and my role as their friend meant the world to me. They shaped how I reach out and love others. Because of them, I have all kinds of friends today. Their roles in my life and mine in theirs made me a better person than I would have been without them. I was known, and loved, as a friend.

I have friends who have waited a long time to be known as a wife. But for some reason that isn't my story. I met John when I was nineteen years old, and our relationship was ridiculously easy. We went on our first date weeks after meeting, and two weeks later we said, "I love you." Less than a year after that he asked me to marry him, and eight months later I was standing in a white dress at the front of a church pledging to love him forever. I was twenty-one when I became a wife, and there was a sense of pride and maturity that came along with being married. To have someone whom I admired and respected and loved so much get to know me— all the parts of me—and then actually want to spend every single day and night for the rest of his life with me was (and is) an inexplicable gift.

But there was one role that didn't come easy: mother. I waited longer than I ever expected to become known as a mom. The tricky thing is that I knew I was a mother long before I felt known as a mother.

I was twenty-two years old when I held a white stick with a purple plus sign in front of my face on a hot summer morning. That was the moment I knew I was a mother. I had been suspiciously hopeful for about a week that a tiny person was growing inside of me, but that little store-bought test confirmed what my heart felt so ready for. I was a mom. I wasn't *going to be* a mom ... I was already the mother of the tiny little being tucked inside my belly.

It was a crisp fall morning when I was wheeled out of the maternity ward with a broken heart and empty arms. The little heart that had beat under mine had suddenly stopped, and no one could tell me why. People struggled to know how to respond to our sudden and unexpected loss. We were so young, and many encouraged us not to worry, that we would be parents someday. I got sympathy cards that read, "Don't worry—you'll be a great mom someday soon!" "Your time will come soon enough, and then you'll get to be a mom!" Those comments were repeated over and over until I realized that the only person who understood that I already was a mother was me.

I didn't feel known anymore, because one of the most important roles in my life was being ignored by everyone

I knew. My pregnancy and baby didn't really count to anyone else because they had never seen my child. But I had carried him day and night. My body had nourished him day and night. My heart had been tied to his day and night. My thoughts toward him had been constant, and everything I did from the moment I saw that purple plus sign had been for his best interest. I was a mother, but no one else seemed to agree because my baby lived in heaven instead of in my arms.

Ronald Reagan once said, "When a child loses his parent, they are called an orphan. When a spouse loses her or his partner, they are called a widow or widower. When parents lose their child, there isn't a word to describe them."

I was in a nameless role. I wore that role like a weighted vest for years.

Meeting Mareto and becoming his mother was a moment of exploding joy and overwhelming relief. All our dreams came true in an instant, and that weighted vest fell off my back. I was suddenly known by the world as a mother, and it was a sweet release from the gnawing ache of being misunderstood for so long. We came home, and everyone started calling me "Mom."

The pediatrician would look up at me in the exam room and ask, "Well, what do you think about this, Mom?" Friends would leave voicemails and texts asking, "How are you doing, Mama?" But there was one person I was waiting on pins and needles for—one person left to call me "Mommy."

Most babies start babbling around six months old and start saying "Mama" and "Dada" between six and twelve months old. By their first birthday most babies know exactly whom they mean when they say, "Mama." But Mareto's first birthday came and went. So did his second. Everything in me was aching to be known by my son.

It was Mareto's speech therapist, Danielle, who first suggested that we work on Mareto learning to call us by name. He was two years old and still communicated like a twelve-month-old, except he never said "Mama" or "Dada." To start, Danielle taught him the words. We sat in her office week after week as she taught him the sounds, asking him to repeat after her on command. Eventually Mareto knew to say "Mama" when told, but he had no idea what the word meant. He'd just repeat it when asked.

Next Danielle explained that we needed to help him understand that people have names the way objects do, and that ours were "Mama" and "Dada." Once he understood that, he would use our names when he needed us.

I remember feeling so emotional just listening to the prospect of Mareto using my name to call for me. What followed were months of exercises. Mareto would spend a minute playing with an iPad, and then I would take it from him and hold it on my lap without making eye contact. He would cry and reach for it, and Danielle would instruct him to say, "Mama." As soon as he repeated the word, I made eye contact with a huge smile and immediately handed him the iPad. We did the same with toys. We hid our faces behind blankets and only popped out when he repeated "Mama" or "Dada."

We spent months doing these exercises at therapy with Danielle and at home with each other. Then one day, without warning, he did it without being asked to repeat the word. When he uttered "Mama" as if it was the easiest thing in the world, we all cheered and clapped and hugged him. He grinned from ear to ear and did it over and over again.

I took the iPad.

"Mama."

(Cheering, clapping, and celebrating.)

I gave the iPad back.

John took the iPad.

"Dada."

(Cheering, clapping, and celebrating.)

John gave the iPad back.

We sat in Danielle's office for thirty minutes repeating the steps above. We went home, and it continued. If I had something that Mareto needed or wanted, he would simply say "Mama." But we didn't yet know if Mareto understood that *I* was Mama or if he thought that *Mama* was the word that magically made toys and iPads and food and cups appear. Until one night . . .

Coming from across the hall and into our room came a tearful, "Mamaaa! Maaaama!" I bolted out of bed and ran to get my little boy out of his crib and comfort his cries. We sat together in the corner chair rocking back and forth as his tears stopped and his breathing deepened. He sighed against my chest and mumbled, "Mama."

I knew then that he knew. He knew I was Mama. He

knew that I would be there for him—to love and comfort and care for him every day. What was already true in both our hearts was now known out loud. It took us about six months from the day we made the goal in speech therapy until the night he whispered my name against my chest. And it felt amazing.

Our names indicate who we are and to whom we belong. Our names and roles give meaning to our relationships and our positions in life. As meaningful and important as all the titles and names I've held in my years on earth are, there is one that is above all others, one that means more than all the others combined. I am a child of God. I am a daughter of the King, adopted into his family, and heir to his kingdom. All other roles will fade and change with the passing of time and the passing of people, but this will never change. And it's brought stability to my searching soul.

The book of Isaiah is a source of reassurance and hope for God's children. I find myself turning to it over and over when I am confused or insecure or hurting. It is a message of salvation and grace to an oppressed and broken people. And nestled within its chapters are expressions of love from God to his people and reassurance that we are known, by name, by our Father. He urges us, "Fear not, for I have redeemed you; I have called you by name, you are mine" (43:1).

And later, in Isaiah 49:16, God tells us, "Behold, I have engraved you on the palms of my hands." Other versions say that God has written your name on the palms of his hands. Not only does God call us by name, but we are etched into him. Who we are is permanently affixed to God. We are known, inside out, by name.

On Sunday mornings after worship service, I pick Arsema up from the nursery. Then we head down the hall to the room where Mareto enjoys children's church. When we enter the room Mareto brightens considerably and begins his now predictable introductions.

WHO WE ARE IS PERMANENTLY AFFIXED TO GOD.

"This is my mommy!" he declares as he gestures my way. And then he turns to his sister. In recent days, he has developed a new way of introducing Arsema.

"This is my 'sema!" he tells the room, but he pays the closest attention to the teacher.

"I know!" she inevitably tells him with a smile.

Mareto then wants to know, "Do you love her?" He asks over and over, "This is my 'sema! Do you love her?"

In this, Mareto highlights the basic need in all of us. We want someone to know us—the real us—and to love us. This is the promise God gives us in Isaiah 43:4, when he declares, "You are precious in my eyes, and honored, and I love you." Whenever I hear Mareto do his introductions, it reminds me of this. It points me back to the God who made me, who reassures me that yes, he sees and knows every inch of me—and loves me. There's freedom and peace in being truly known. You and I are not nameless faces in the crowd to God. We are his children, intimately understood, completely accepted, and deeply loved.

seventeen

"You're So Cutie-ful"

It was a gorgeous spring morning, and I woke up feeling awful. Since moms don't often get sick days and the kids were feeling fine and full of energy, we went to the park. I found a bench and settled in to watch them play. Mareto came to tell me he was headed for the swing set, and I called out, "I love you!" as he turned to run.

He stopped and turned, without skipping a beat, to respond, "I love you. You're so cutie-ful, Mommy."

As I watched him run off to swing, tears filled my eyes. I wasn't running or chasing or laughing and playing like some of the other moms at the park. My body ached, my head throbbed, and I was exhausted. I wasn't at my best, but I was at the park. And to Mareto, I was completely and fully enough because I am his.

We live in a culture that screams "more, more, more!" at

162

us every day. *More* has permeated every aspect of our lives so that it's no longer about not *having* enough; we now believe that *we* aren't enough. Supposedly John D. Rockefeller was once asked, "How much money is enough money?" and his response was, "Just a little bit more."

We believe that about ourselves too. That if we were just a little thinner, a little more successful, a little smarter, a little more ambitious, or talented, or connected, then we would be enough. We are perpetually dissatisfied and insecure about who we are and what we do.

A few years ago *Time* magazine ran a story about attachment parenting. On the cover of the magazine a slender blonde woman stood with one hand on her hip staring confidently into the camera. In front of her stood her four-year-old son on a chair, breastfeeding. The cover asked in bold red letters, "Are You Mom Enough?" It caused an uproar.

I'll admit that my initial reaction to the cover was one of anger and offense, just like many other women. Even though John and I practice some aspects of attachment parenting, we don't subscribe to it all; and I never breast-fed my children for a single day, let alone for four years. Was I supposed to assume I wasn't a good enough mom? The simple answer is, of course not. Do I think the headline was a poor decision? Yes. Do I think the mom on the cover would question whether or not I am a good enough mom? No.

So I wondered why I and many other women had such a strong reaction to a cover suggesting that we're not enough.

And the answer was uncomfortable and obvious: because I didn't have the confidence in myself.

You see, when we really believe that who we are is enough, then offensive headlines don't rattle us. Instead we see them for how ridiculous and false they are. We can chuckle and shake our heads, or even feel a bit of sadness and compassion for the ones who really believe it. It doesn't knock us off course or reignite the "mommy wars." But that's only possible if we really believe that who we are is enough.

We're overwhelmed with mom-guilt at every turn. Advertisers use it to their advantage, using phrases like, "Moms who want to do what's best for their babies use (insert product)," implying that moms who don't use their product either a) don't know what's best for their children, or b) don't care to do what's best for their children.

Instead of arguing over whose method is best or right and who is doing a good enough job, I wish we'd channel that energy into highlighting the wonderful things in each of the parenting styles we moms use and make this world a friendlier and safer place for moms in general.

Instead of arguing over breast versus bottle, I wish we'd recognize how privileged we are that we even get to make that choice. Let's put our energy into making sure every mother everywhere can feed her baby.

Instead of battling about homeschool versus public school versus private school versus Montessori, I wish we'd join hands to make education accessible, meaningful, fun, interesting, and safe for all children everywhere in the world.

Instead of judging the mom hovering over her toddler at the park or sitting on the bench looking at her iPhone, I wish we'd chat more and smile more and high-five each other for getting out of the house on a sunny afternoon. I wish we'd recognize that there are women in the world who live in war zones and can't let their children go outside, let alone drive five miles down the road to a nice (free) playground.

When we aren't enough, no one is enough—and we duke it out to prove ourselves.

Moms aren't the only ones susceptible to this insecurity. In the years before I became a mother, I struggled with feeling like I wasn't enough because I didn't have children. I kept hearing messages about how the most valuable role a woman will fill is that of mother. Christian circles elevated motherhood as a woman's "highest calling," which left me feeling unimportant, unneeded, and not enough.

> WHEN WE AREN'T ENOUGH, NO ONE IS ENOUGH—AND WE DUKE IT OUT TO PROVE OURSELVES.

I wish I had recognized the lies then. I wish I'd known then that a woman's (and man's) highest calling is being a child of God. I wish I'd believed that it wasn't the roles I filled or didn't fill that gave me value, but rather God who gives me value. He, the One who created every part of who I am, determined from day one that I am already enough.

Unfortunately, the same battle between the truth and

lies about being enough or not enough has filtered down to my children.

April is designated as "Autism Awareness Month," and campaigns such as "light it up blue" encourage people to wear blue clothing and blue ribbons and put blue bulbs in their porch lights to raise awareness about autism. It seems harmless, but this month also comes with its own side of debate and backlash.

Articles circulate the internet encouraging parents to recognize the signs of autism in their children. Then follow-up articles explain how to prevent autism. Then countless studies and articles try to explain what causes autism. Then some groups even claim they know how to cure autism. And in the end, instead of raising awareness—or the more important goal of acceptance—we breed division and offense within the autism community itself.

I've been the author of a number of articles about autism awareness and acceptance. I've read countless others, and from what I can tell, the debate stems from people within the community holding two very different views. One group feels autism is an illness that can be cured and, if not, then it's a very sad and tragic situation for the individuals with autism and their families. The other group feels that autism isn't a disability at all, but rather a difference in how the brain works and experiences the world. They say a cure isn't needed (or possible), because autism is so much of who that person is.

I understand both groups. I identify more with one than

the other, but I can see why each one holds the views they do. To me, as a mother who is raising a child on the autism spectrum, to suggest that his autism needs to be "cured" feels hurtful and insulting. Mareto is unique and amazing and sees the world in ways I don't. I need his perspective on life, and I think the world needs more people like him. Autism is a part of who he is, not a disease to be eradicated. Does it mean he faces more challenges than the average five-year-old? Yes. Are we up for it? Yes.

I've read many blogs and books written by adults on the autism spectrum. I've watched documentaries and interviews as well, and the overwhelming message I hear from these individuals is that they are incredibly happy with who they are. They feel that they are enough—as autistic people. I agree.

It's easier for me to come to this conclusion than for other parents, and I understand that. My son doesn't have multiple seizures a day. He has speech, he isn't prone to fits of violent rage, and he hasn't yet experienced especially cruel and brutal bullying. I understand why some parents feel their children would be better off without autism, and I understand that view comes from a place of both fear and love. But I also think it's hurting us as a society.

To focus so much energy on figuring out the cause or cure for autism takes away from the more important work of raising awareness and acceptance for all individuals, autistic or not. Rather than wonder if someone should or shouldn't be the way they are, I wish we'd all assume that each of us is unique and is here on this earth because we have something to offer.

Instead of researching causes, I wish we'd put more time and money into early intervention and training therapists. I wish help centers were accessible to parents and children or anyone who needs them.

Instead of writing yet another article about whether or not vaccines cause autism, I wish we'd write investigative pieces about the special education programs in our public school systems and implement improvements.

Instead of fighting about how to cure autism, I wish we'd sit down and have meaningful discussions about how best to support individuals on the spectrum who are making the transition into adulthood.

Because when we all start believing that we are each enough as is, we will start exploring ways to live fully and to help others do the same. There is freedom and grace and compassion and love in knowing that who we are is enough, but it only works when we believe it of others as well. When we say that every individual is enough, what we are really acknowledging is that God has made every person to be wonderful.

There's a bit of bristling sometimes in the Christian community about the term *enough*. I've seen my share of angry tweets and blog posts declaring that we are not and never will be enough, and that is precisely why we need Jesus. I agree, and I disagree. I think it depends on what we're saying we're *enough* for.

Am I enough to save mankind? Of course not. I'm not enough for someone else's job and calling either, because it wasn't what I was created for. But I rest solely in the confidence of the God who created me and designed me for my own unique purposes. I rest in the God who designed Mareto and pieced together his brain exactly as intended.

Take a quick skim of Psalm 139. You might already have it memorized; maybe you jot it in cards before sending them off to friends expecting babies. Read it again, and insert your name in verses 13–18. I'm going to do it below with my son's name.

> For you formed Mareto's inward parts; you knitted him together in his mother's womb. I praise you, for Mareto is fearfully and wonderfully made. Wonderful are your works; my soul knows it very well. Mareto's frame was not hidden from you, when he was being made in secret, intricately woven in the depths of the earth. Your eyes saw his unformed substance; in your book were written, every one of them, the days that were formed for him, when as yet there was none of them. How precious to me are your thoughts, O God! How vast is the sum of them! If I would count them, they are more than the sand. Mareto awakes, and he is still with you.

There were absolutely no accidents when God dreamed up Mareto. There were no mistakes made when he was being formed. When God started writing his story for Mareto in the books, he knew that it would include autism and that it would have purpose. And when he thinks about Mareto, which he does constantly, he thinks about what a wonderfully unique and special little boy he is. Mareto is enough, because God is enough.

Friends, that is true for you. I hope you put your name in those verses and saw that whatever it is that you don't like about you or whatever you wish you could change is enough.

I hope you saw that God loves you right now as is. I hope you know deep down that you are unique and special and created with a purpose only you can fill.

I've heard it said that when everyone's special, then nobody's special. The saying gets tossed around a lot when talking about parenting and the "everybody gets a trophy" mentality. I disagree because when everyone is special, then everyone is special. When everyone is unique, then everyone is unique. And when everyone is enough, then we can stop being distracted by judging who is and isn't and get down to making this world a better place.

When I believe I'm enough, I

> WHEN EVERYONE IS ENOUGH, THEN WE CAN STOP BEING DISTRACTED BY JUDGING WHO IS AND ISN'T AND GET DOWN TO MAKING THIS WORLD A BETTER PLACE.

can relax at the park and enjoy watching my kids run and play, or answer texts that come through without shame. When I believe that I am enough, I can fix a home-cooked meal or order a pizza to be delivered without guilt. When I believe I am enough as is, I can start the project or invite my friends over for coffee.

When the world believes Mareto is enough, he won't sit in a classroom under the weight of the expectation that he conform to one way of learning. When the world believes Mareto is enough, he will have opportunities for relationships unhindered by silent (or not so silent) assumptions and judgments. When the world believes Mareto is enough, he won't be accepted in spite of his differences but because of them and all the light he brings to the world.

If we could view ourselves and others the way God views us, we'd all be a little less ready to argue, a little less offended, a little less harsh, and a little less judgmental. We'd know just how much we have to offer this world and open ourselves up to running headfirst into those callings. We'd feel safe and secure and confident. We would celebrate each other and help each other and love each other better. We would trust God more and have more hope for a better world.

God loves us right now. Our value isn't dependent on our actions or our offerings, but on the fact that he created us to love him and be with him forever. We don't need to tie our significance as people to anything other than the God who created us. The equation isn't Mareto +/-autism = enough, and it isn't Lauren +/-anything = enough, and it isn't you +/-anything = enough. It is just us and God . . . and we are enough.

There's freedom in believing that equation. It's amazing how opening our hearts up to this truth—that we are all cutie-ful just as we are—colors everything else in our lives. In the end, it's not what you do, but who you are that matters. Who you are is enough. And you are cutie-ful.

eighteen

"CHEESE AND CRACKERS!"

Mareto was just three years old when he found my fancy camera on the kitchen counter. It had been a Mother's Day gift from John, and I was extremely careful and picky about who could touch that camera. We'd moved from Virginia Beach to Lexington just a few weeks earlier, and we were still getting settled into our new home. I had the camera out because I was taking as many pictures as I could, documenting special "firsts" with the kids in this new place to send to the family we'd left behind in our move.

One morning I rounded the corner of the dining room to find Mareto looking through the viewfinder. There was something about him that made me stop short of rushing over to grab the camera out of his hands. I watched silently while he swayed a little and then, breathing deeply, he let out a whispered, "Cheese and crackers!" as he snapped his first photograph. I was a bit entranced by his careful and thoughtful demeanor.

I stood, leaning against the wall, and watched him repeat this cycle several times. Swaying, searching, breathing out, "Cheese and crackers!" and then snap, he'd click the button to capture an image.

When Mareto grew tired of taking pictures, he gently placed the camera on the floor and walked away. I quickly ran over to look through the photos he'd taken and was in awe of the sweet and simple beauty of each of them. Some were blurry and some were crystal clear, but he had uncovered an unmistakable gift of art that we encourage today.

Mareto has continued to take pictures as he feels like it, and I have learned not to worry so much about little hands using my fancy camera. The results have been remarkable, and some of the most breathtaking pictures I've ever seen have come from Mareto's curiosity and creativity.

As I've watched Mareto explore this creative gift and take joy in capturing images, I am struck by how easy it is for him. With each new picture he snaps, I hear, "Cheese and crackers!" Sometimes he whispers it like a gentle reminder, and other times he loudly declares it in a singsongy voice. It's a lighthearted and silly phrase that makes him laugh and brings him happiness. And when he blurts it out before every photograph, that same joy comes through in his art. Mareto isn't worrying about whether or not he is good enough or qualified to be a photographer. He's simply having fun.

Each of us has a creative spirit, but we need the right

environment and tools to discover and grow our gifts. It could be photography, painting, music, or writing. Or maybe it's chemistry, engineering, or marine biology. We all have something inside that lights us up, stirs up our passion, and frees our hearts when we let it out.

We each have special gifts and creative sparks that make this world a better and more beautiful place. We each have something to contribute, but sometimes we have trouble believing that. Sometimes we squelch our gifts because we don't believe they are good enough or worthwhile. Sometimes we feel silly or maybe even worry that it's arrogant to believe we're creatively gifted and have something to offer.

I love the way Elizabeth Gilbert addressed this issue in her recent bestseller *Big Magic*. She said that this belief that we are free to create and offer to the world is the opposite of arrogance, and that it "will actually *take you out of yourself* and allow you to engage more fully with life. Because often what keeps you from creative living *is* your self-absorption (your self-doubt, your self-disgust, your self-judgment, your crushing sense of self-protection)."[1]

You might not be the best in the world at whatever creative outlet you pursue, but I can promise you this: You are the absolute best at doing it the way you do it. You are unique, and no one else can create the exact way you do.

But fear holds us back. Chasing perfection leaves us paralyzed, because it's a completely unattainable goal. I'm not sure why we chase perfection to begin with, since it seems to be widely accepted that the imperfections are what make things special and beautiful. It's the difference between a paint-by-numbers portrait and a Vincent van Gogh.

I love the subtitle of Myquillyn Smith's home-decorating book, *The Nesting Place*. It's really the message of her whole book: *It Doesn't Have to Be Perfect to Be Beautiful.* Myquillyn encourages readers to let go of the idea of perfection and embrace the goal of lived-in beauty. When she was able to embrace this herself, it led to a sense of fun and freedom in her own life. And when a designer friend whom she greatly admires walked into Myquillyn's home for the first time, this happened: "She looked around smiling and declared, 'Everything is just a little bit off.' She had no idea what a huge compliment that was to me."[2]

My mother took up oil painting a few years ago, and the whole family is in awe of her talent. She started with painting tutorials she found online or in books. One of her first paintings done this way was supposed to be a painting of a couple walking along the coastline. But Mom didn't like the way the couple looked. In fact, she didn't like people in her painting at all. She decided to paint over them and instead, where people "should" be, there is now a walrus. It's gorgeous. It doesn't look like the image she was "supposed to" create; it's better.

My mom didn't ask permission to change her painting, just like Mareto didn't ask permission to take pictures. They simply created something because they wanted to, and the end result was joy and satisfaction in their work.

A few months after I noticed Mareto's interest in photography, I put together a blog post with several of his pictures. The response was amazing; people from all over the world emailed and messaged me to tell me how moved they were by his gift. Professional photographers told me that he has an incredible eye for light and beauty. I received an email requesting to use some of his photography for an art exhibit in Paris.

This is what happens when we freely create. Mareto wasn't worried about getting it right or capturing the perfect photograph. He was simply taking pictures of things he found interesting and valuable. He snapped pictures uninhibited by self-imposed expectations and fears of failure. He did it because it was fun and brought him joy. And that came through in his pictures.

Was every picture perfect? Of course not. Some were extremely blurry, and some were overexposed. But mixed in those outtakes were little treasures. A particularly striking image was captured shortly after the kids woke one morning. The living room was still fairly dark, and the sun was just beginning to stream through the blinds. Mareto lifted the camera, aimed it at his sister, whispered "cheese and crackers," and took a picture. It is stunning. One photographer told me he wished he had taken the image because it was so incredible. Mareto wasn't thinking about it; he was just doing what felt right.

Perhaps you aren't an artist, but you are something else. Your creativity might come out in other ways, like my sister's love for animals and how I'm now convinced she's the greatest gift to the veterinary clinic she works for. Or like my brother, who has a brilliant critical mind and just accepted a highly sought-after internship with the United Nations. (Yes, the actual UN in New York City.) Or maybe you're like my sister-in-law, who bakes the most delicious desserts, or my brother-in-law, who puts his heart and creativity into his backyard garden. Maybe you're an office manager who just came up with a more efficient way to run things, or a teacher who finger paints and acts out children's books with hilarious voices. You don't have to be the stereotypical version of creative. But don't ever think you're not creative at all.

How do I know you have it in you? Because I know who made you.

The entirety of Scripture starts with a simple statement: "In the beginning, God created the heavens and the earth" (Genesis 1:1).

Then the story describes everything God created: the light and the dark, the water and the land, the plants and the animals, the sun and the moon, and the fish and the birds. He saved you and me for last.

Genesis 1:26 says, "Then God said, 'Let us make man in our image, after our likeness.'" This was God's intention. He thought it, and then he did it.

"So God created man in his own image, in the image of God he created him; male and female he created them" (v. 27).

In the space of two verses we are told four times that we are created in God's image, created by God to be like God.

Not to be God, but made in his likeness. We are to emulate the facets of who God is, and one of the most recognizable facets of God is creativity. We call him that by name—the Creator. Our Creator.

That's how I know you are creative and that it already lives inside of you. The day you were born you held deep within you all the tools and gifts you need to create in exactly the way you are supposed to.

It's why shepherds played harps and wrote songs under the night sky. It's why explorers drew maps and kept logs and sailed the seas. It's why carpenters made cathedral doors and Jane Austen wrote books. It's why engineers design bridges and why we have electricity and indoor plumbing today.

I've told people that I discovered writing by accident. In 2009 I started a blog to process some changes in my life, and eventually I started reading other blogs and became part of a growing online community. People started reading my blog, and over the years it grew. That led to an idea that maybe I could write a book. And a few years after I verbalized that dream,

> THE DAY YOU WERE BORN YOU HELD DEEP WITHIN YOU ALL THE TOOLS AND GIFTS YOU NEED TO CREATE IN EXACTLY THE WAY YOU ARE SUPPOSED TO.

I signed with an agent, put together a proposal, and was offered a publishing contract. But the whole "by accident" part of it—that's not really true.

The truth is that I was in seventh grade when the idea of being an author first entered my mind. My social studies teacher, Mrs. Lipsey, noticed my unusual level of interest in Civil War history. I don't mean battle tactics and plans (although I certainly learned more about that than I wanted to when my parents dragged us to every battlefield within driving distance of our Virginia home). I was interested in Clara Barton and Harriet Beecher Stowe and Sojourner Truth and Harriet Tubman. I was interested in the stories of the soldiers and their families, of the politicians and their backgrounds, and the reasons they made the choices they did. I wanted to know the *why* more than the *how*. I wanted to hear and read and interpret the stories behind the era that simultaneously left me intrigued and heartbroken.

In my yearbook that June, Mrs. Lipsey wrote a simple message: "Lauren, one day I think you'll write a Civil War history book."

She'll probably never know how much that sentence meant to me. The idea that I could write a book wasn't initially sparked when people started reading my blog. It was sparked the day someone saw an interest and a gift in me and pointed it out. Throughout high school I kept journals of poems and short stories I wrote. In college I majored in history and political science but took as many literature and creative writing classes as I could fit into my schedule.

And then a funny thing happened. To graduate from Old Dominion University, every student must take an exit exam. It's different based on your degree path, but since mine was liberal arts, my exit exam was to choose one of three writing prompts and write an essay in the allotted time. I was thrilled. I loved to write—it's why I did well in my degree plan. History exams are mainly in essay form—so I thought this would be a breeze.

I went into the testing center and received my sheet with the prompts on it. They were extremely generic, and I don't remember which prompt I chose. But I wrote my essay and turned it in with time to spare. I felt confident and was looking forward to graduating at the end of the semester. Then I got an email saying I had failed the exit exam. I was shocked!

Thankfully, I was able to meet with the people at the testing center to find out why I had failed. I hadn't used commas appropriately, and that was the sole reason for my failing grade. They showed me my essay with all the places where commas should and shouldn't have been, and as they tallied the number of comma errors, they explained that it simply surpassed the number allowed to pass.

I rescheduled my exam for later in the semester and met with one of my English professors weekly to nail down exactly where to enter my commas. I went into the second exam feeling anything but confident; I suddenly couldn't remember the "rules of writing" and had a bad feeling my punctuation would be off again. I sat down and picked yet another generic writing prompt. This one I remember: we had to write an essay about our favorite song.

I took up every minute of the allotted time. I struggled to get even the introduction paragraph out because I kept rereading it, unsure if my commas were well placed. I looked at the clock and realized that if I kept up this pace I would never finish the essay on time, so I made a decision: I would just write the essay in its entirety and then go back and fix all the punctuation. But I still felt frozen at the end of each sentence, too worried about those silly commas. So I made another decision: I would just write short sentences. If very few of my sentences needed commas, then my rate of error would be lower and I just might pass and be able to collect my diploma.

That was the most poorly written thing I've probably ever created. It was choppy and lacking any real heart. I read it out loud to myself, and it sounded robotic and detached. If this was supposed to be an essay about why I loved this particular song, I sure couldn't tell. It sounded as if I had no feelings invested in it whatsoever. I turned it in, disappointed because I was out of time.

A week later I got an email. I had passed. I had met the level of perfection the school was looking for, but the paper itself was awful. I had been so worried about meeting an expectation that what I had actually written wasn't me at all. I was proud I had passed and would now get my degree, but I wasn't proud of my essay. I didn't write anything but letters and emails for the next four years.

Then I started my blog. The blogging world doesn't care about commas, and I didn't care about commas because I had zero audience when I started writing. I wrote for me. Even after months the only person reading my words was my husband, and I was fine with that. When people did start reading my blog, they didn't comment on my flawed punctuation but rather on the content of my posts—because I was creating freely with no fear or expectations of perfection. I was simply sitting down in front of my computer and letting my fingers fall on the keyboard and the words pour out the way Mareto breathes out, "cheese and crackers" while snapping a photograph.

My blog audience has grown over the years to become larger than anything I would have expected when I first started writing just for me. I can be tempted to freeze up in fear when people leave hurtful comments or say cruel things in response to an article I've written, but we don't create because we need praise and we don't create to attain a goal of perfection. We create because it's who we are. So I take my cues from Mareto's little hands holding my big camera.

Watching Mareto not overthink or worry about perfection has encouraged me to do the same. Instead of obsessing over a flawless end product, may we embrace the freedom to simply breathe in and whisper out "cheese and crackers" as we release our gifts into the world. We create because it's in us. We create because God made us that way.

nineteen

"It's a Job-a-doo!"

Each and every day that I pick Mareto up from school, I ask his teachers or the aide if he had a good day. A few weeks ago I didn't even need to ask. I saw the joy on Mareto's face as he bounded out the door and into my arms for our standard reunion hug. We got buckled into the car, and he couldn't wait to tell me about his day.

"I was the leader today!" he exclaimed with a sweet mixture of delight and pride.

"You were?! That's so great, buddy!" I responded with equal excitement.

He then went on to explain that he had been the line leader at school. It was his job to be at the front of the line for recess and any other trips they might take—to the library, the bathroom, music, or movement class. Mareto was given an important job to do that day, and he was filled with pride over the responsibility. I later found out that it was actually a reward. Mareto had sat in his seat at the table for the entire duration of snack time (which is quite difficult for him), and he was rewarded with the job of line leader.

Imagine that, being rewarded with work. And not only being given work as a reward, but also viewing it that way. Mareto was elated that he had a special job, and he took it very seriously. The same goes for us at home. When I need the kids to get involved with something, I say, "Will you be my helper today?" or "I have an important job for you. Do you think you can help Mommy do it?" Then I watch Mareto stand up a little straighter, chest puffed out in confidence and eyes wide open with excitement before he lets out, "It's a job-a-doo!"

When it's time to pick up toys, wash hands, get dressed, or any number of the responsibilities we're working on teaching our son, we love to hear, "It's a job-a-doo!" He utters the phrase with enthusiasm as he bounces off to take on the task at hand. It's both amusing and humbling to witness. We laughed the first time we heard it because the phrase is so cute. We knew he'd picked it up from something he heard and then twisted it to make it his own. And I am inspired by his joyful attitude toward work, his welcoming spirit toward responsibility.

I don't always have the same attitude toward my responsibilities.

It's one thing doing a job I absolutely love—like writing, for instance. Each time a magazine or website asks if

I'd be willing to write an article, I grin from ear to ear and inwardly declare, "It's a job-a-doo!" When I got offered my publishing contract for this book, I nearly did a cartwheel. (I mean, I didn't because I didn't want to end up in the ER, but I wanted to!) Writing is my equivalent of being the line leader in preschool.

But what about my other responsibilities? I don't always stand up straight and bound off to do the dishes or fold the laundry. I've been known to grumble and complain about cleaning the toilets and unclogging the shower drain. And sometimes I wish we didn't need to eat every single day. I could really go for a cooking-once-a-week schedule. Those jobs don't feel exciting. Those jobs feel mundane and tedious. Those jobs are also incredibly necessary.

I've noticed something interesting about myself over the years: When my home is in order I am generally happier and more productive. When the dishes are done and my kitchen counters are clean and shiny, when the laundry is folded and put away, when the beds are all made, the floors are clean, each room is tidy, and the surfaces have been dusted, I am ready to conquer the world. When my environment is organized, my brain follows suit and my attitude gets a huge boost. Of course, what that means is that the jobs (laundry, dishes, mopping, etc.) that I feel are so wearisome are actually quite underrated and an integral part of my mental and emotional well-being.

Doing the laundry makes me a better writer. Keeping the kitchen clean and the living room tidy makes me a better friend. Keeping the beds made and the pantry stocked makes me a better spouse and a better mom. Because when the "little" things are taken care of, I am more focused during my writing time, I am organized and open to friends stopping by, and I am content and happy at the end of the day when the kids are running crazy through the house and I am putting dinner on the table. Those little jobs aren't so little after all.

There's no such thing as unimportant work. We need the plumber every bit as much as we need the CEO. We need the janitor and the trash collector just as much as we need the surgeon and the teacher. We've gotten into a habit of creating a totem pole of value for various jobs, and it's affected our attitude toward work in general.

In a recent article for the *New York Post*, Ivana Trump defended and sought to clarify her ex-husband Donald Trump's thoughts on immigration. There was a public outcry when the article quoted her saying, "As long as you come here legally and get a proper job . . . we need immigrants. Who's going to vacuum our living rooms and clean up after us? Americans don't like to do that."[1]

THERE'S NO SUCH THING AS UNIMPORTANT WORK.

There's a lot wrong with those sentences—the idea that immigrants are only good for cleaning up after Americans being at the top of that list. But you know what? That last sentence is true.

We don't like to vacuum and clean up after ourselves. We don't like to do the jobs that feel dirty and meaningless. And because we view those jobs as menial and insignificant, we transfer those views to the people who do them as a vocation. The result is arrogant and elitist attitudes like the one above.

Let's just imagine for a moment that every trash collector, janitor, dishwasher, plumber, and electrician quit their job tomorrow. Things would come to a grinding halt because their jobs are valuable and meaningful. All our work has purpose and contributes to life more than we may realize. Sometimes we will see the return for our work and why it mattered, and other times we'll never see its impact on the world and the people around us. But it's all important and it all matters, because every job we do contributes to life and ministry.

Several years ago my friend Andrea founded the Created for Care ministry. After going to one of the retreats simply as an attendee, I knew I wanted to get involved. Later that year I sent Andrea a text telling her that I would love to help out in any area that had a need. She almost immediately responded to tell me they needed a break-out speaker to talk about infertility at their next retreat. It wasn't what I'd had in mind (I was thinking more along the lines of helping out at the registration table), but I prayed about it and nervously agreed. Months later I helped redesign their website, and soon Andrea was asking me to join the team as their web manager. I was overjoyed.

About a year later I got another phone call. The team needed someone to run the computers for the retreat weekends. This is a job that seems small and not too exciting. It involves spending hours before the retreats putting together slides and videos in ProPresenter and creating playlists. I won't bore you with the prep details, but a lot goes into things before we even start an event. I spent most of my time over the weekend of that year's retreat in the sound booth behind the computer screen, clicking "Next" for every worship slide so that attendees could sing along with the worship team. I put up the welcome screen and played music while women were coming and going for main sessions and break-outs. I ran the slides for every session and played videos when they were called for. And I did it all in a little black booth in the back left-hand corner of a room filled with five hundred women.

One year Andrea and I were sitting in that booth around three o'clock in the morning getting everything ready for the event beginning at two o'clock that afternoon. We were having some technical issues, and I'm sure our delirious exhaustion wasn't helping matters. We started chatting about the ministry in general and everyone's role in putting on each retreat. Andrea looked me right in the eye and said, "Thank you for taking this on. No one wants to do this job."

And I responded in total seriousness, "When I offered to help I truly meant that I would help in any way you needed it. If you had told me that you needed someone to clean the bathrooms, I would have done it. Because I believe so much in what this ministry is doing."

It strikes me as odd that I felt that way about cleaning bathrooms at Created for Care but not so much in my own home. The difference was that I could see so clearly the impact a single Created for Care weekend had on these women (and myself). It was like a year's worth of pouring into hearts and lives had been condensed into one weekend, and the results were abundantly obvious. I couldn't see those same results in my own home. We don't see the impact that daily laundry and dishes and toilet scrubbing have on our family in quite the same magnitude. But it's there whether we see it or not.

The funny thing is that every year the Created for Care team gets tons of emails from women asking to help out. And we always respond that we need more volunteers! But when we tell them that we need help with things like setting up and breaking down, manning the bookstore and registration table, or sitting in on sessions and recording them for our audio sale, they aren't as interested anymore. We realize that most of these women want speaking gigs or big, up-front jobs. They don't want to do the "little" tasks. But what we tend to often forget or don't fully understand is that there is no "big work" or "little work."

In 1 Corinthians 12:14–20 Paul uses our own bodies to illustrate this point.

> For the body does not consist of one member but of many. If the foot should say, "Because I am not a hand, I do not belong to the body," that would not make it any less a part

of the body. And if the ear should say, "Because I am not an eye, I do not belong to the body," that would not make it any less a part of the body. If the whole body were an eye, where would be the sense of hearing? If the whole body were an ear, where would be the sense of smell? But as it is, God arranged the members in the body, each one of them, as he chose. If all were a single member, where would the body be? As it is, there are many parts, yet one body.

We can't all be the CEO of a large company, and we weren't all meant to be. The CEO is no more necessary than the janitor who comes to clean each night and the secretary who answers and transfers calls throughout the day. In fact, the CEO can only do his or her job *because of* the janitor and the secretary and a whole bunch of other people. Our work matters, whether we view it as big or small, because all work is service to others and all work keeps life moving.

My family spends more than a typical amount of time in doctors' offices and hospitals. It's not good and it's not bad; it's just our normal. My daughter is getting ready to have her fifth surgery in three

OUR WORK MATTERS, WHETHER WE VIEW IT AS BIG OR SMALL, BECAUSE ALL WORK IS SERVICE TO OTHERS AND ALL WORK KEEPS LIFE MOVING.

years, but Mareto was actually the first of our children to need surgery. He was sixteen months old at the time, and I was terrified. Both John and I had gone under the knife a few different times for various reasons, but it's a completely different experience to watch your child go in for an operation.

When the nurse came to get Mareto to take him to the operating room, I tried so hard to keep it together. I smiled big and squeezed him tight. I told him he was amazing and strong and that this sweet nurse was going to be his very best friend. I told him that he was just going to take a little nap, and we'd be there as soon as he woke up. And then that sweet nurse took my baby boy from my arms and walked away. As they rounded the corner I turned my face into John's chest and bawled in the hallway.

A few minutes later I dried my tears, and we walked into the waiting room designated for parents. An older woman sat behind the sign-in table, and after we wrote our names down, she smiled up at me and asked if I'd like to take a bear. I hadn't even noticed the box filled with little homemade and hand-stitched teddy bears. We carefully picked out a bear made of blue fabric and sat down to stare at a screen that displayed ID numbers and status updates. I looked at Mareto's number and waited for his status to move from "OR" to "Recovery." It might sound silly, but holding that little bear and knowing I would give it to my son later that day made me feel a little better. It was a small comfort amid a hard moment.

We've repeated this scene four times, and next month

we'll do it again. A nurse will come and take Arsema from my arms. I will smile and show my brave face until she rounds the corner, and then I will cry in the hallway. But I know that after I compose myself I'll walk down the hall and pick out a bear, likely one with pink flowers, and I'll hold it on my lap while I stare at Arsema's number on the screen. And the comfort that little bear brings will make a heart-wrenching and anxiety-filled day a whole lot better.

I don't know if the people who stitch those bears know the value of their work. I don't know if they realize just how important it is to us parents sitting in the waiting room. Because the people who make those bears have impacted my life and my heart just as much as the nurses and doctors and surgeons who have skillfully and tenderly cared for my children. I hope they know, and I hope they find joy in their work. I have a feeling they do, because most people don't sit at home hand-stitching little bears unless they know it matters.

Even if we don't see that our work matters, and even if no one shows us their appreciation or tells us the impact our work has made on their life, we still need to do our jobs full of heart and full of joy. Colossians 3:23 tells us, "Whatever you do, work at it with all your heart, as working for the Lord, not for human masters" (NIV).

Work at it with all your heart. I am so convicted by this verse. I am not working with my whole heart when I complain about the dishes or the laundry or volunteering at church or my children's school. Working with your whole heart looks like Mareto crying out, "It's a job-a-doo!" when I

193

tell him to wash his hands before dinner or put his jacket on the hook in the foyer. Working with your whole heart is my children standing up a little taller and grinning from ear to ear when I give them bags of groceries to help me carry from the car to the house.

It seems like such a simple lesson: to love the work you do and do the work you love. But when we feel unfulfilled, unimportant, or underappreciated, it becomes hard for us to find that joy in our work. Watching Mareto take joy in building a bridge or washing his hands has shown me that there is no "small" work in this life. Everything we do matters, and when we begin to realize that, our attitude turns from grumbling to joy. A joyous attitude produces joyous work, which changes not only our own heart but also those around us. Let's roll up our sleeves and get to work because "It's a job-a-doo!"

twenty

"TODAY IS MY BIRTHDAY!"

One of my favorite things about Mareto is his capacity for joy and celebration. When he gets especially excited he lets out this squeaky "Yesss!" or sometimes even says, "I'm so ah-sited!" And the wonderful thing about it is that it doesn't take too much to get him excited. He can get all worked up over one Oreo cookie to the same degree that I might express my excitement over Christmas. It's so sweet and innocent... and honest.

This happened recently one random Tuesday. The weather was nice, so after Arsema's nap I decided it was a good day for the playground. When she padded downstairs, holding her teddy bear and her blanket, I announced, "Guess what time it is? It's time for the playground!"

Arsema's eyes brightened, and she ran to get her sneakers. Mareto pumped his fist in the air and yelled, "Yesss!" We gathered our things and climbed in our blue minivan.

There are a few playgrounds in our small city. One sits at the end of my friend Rachel's street. I like it because it's small and doesn't have too much equipment, and I can sit on a bench and see the kids at all times. The other is part of the local middle school but is open to anyone. It's a bit bigger, but I still have clear visibility of my children at all times and can watch them from a bench or a blanket on the grass. A trip to these playgrounds is either relaxing because I can read or simply sit in my own thoughts or fun because I'm meeting friends and we can actually sit in one place and chat while keeping an eye on our kids.

Then there's the playground my kids love. They have named it "the Big-Big Playground," and it is their favorite. There are swings (two different sets, including one tire swing) and numerous slides. There are zip lines and monkey bars and a sandbox. This playground has a shaky bridge and tons of little forts and steps and hiding places—which is precisely why I don't love this playground. I can never sit in one place when we come to the Big-Big Playground. I spend my time running around and making sure I know where the kids are, occasionally shouting out their names when I can't find them. There are two exits, and you can't watch both at once while also keeping an eye on your kids. It's exhausting for me and over-the-top fun for them. Go figure.

This particular day I decided we could go to the Big-Big Playground. We left our neighborhood, and I turned out onto the main road. The kids were extra chatty in the backseat, and as we drove along they asked repeatedly, "Which playground are we going to, Mommy?" I just told them we'd have to wait and see. A few minutes later I turned left onto the road leading to the Big-Big Playground, and Mareto knew.

"Yesss!" I heard from the back. Then he started singing, "Today is my birthday! Today is my birthday!"

Mareto deals in extremes. A trip to the playground is equivalent to a birthday party for Mareto, but the wings popping off his Buzz Lightyear toy means Christmas is ruined.

I see a lot of myself in the "Christmas is ruined" side of Mareto, but not as much in the "Today is my birthday!" side. Little things trip me up and put me in a funk for the rest of the day, but all Mareto needs is an Oreo or a quick trip to the playground to turn a bad day into the best day ever. I see this as both a lesson and a challenge to me: to view every day as a gift.

It can be easier to say that every day is a gift from God than to really believe it. After all, not every day is filled with trips to our favorite playground or Oreos after lunch. Some days are really awful and it's hard to find things to bring us joy, but they are right there in the smallest details just waiting to be celebrated.

While I was writing this book I had a total hysterectomy. This was a surgery we had prayed about for more than a year before coming to the conclusion that it was my only option for better health and well-being. The day of my surgery felt big and scary, and I just wanted to blink and have it behind me. I didn't exactly check into the hospital looking for things to celebrate.

The surgery itself went well, and the first twenty-four

hours of recovery seemed to be going smoothly with the exception of a few hiccups. But then it all fell apart. My second night home the pain came crashing down on me and didn't seem manageable. By three a.m. I was bent over the bed crying. Seven hours later my husband was driving ninety miles per hour down the interstate toward the hospital while I screamed and moaned from the passenger seat.

I was mentally, emotionally, and spiritually drained. My mom kept the kids with her while I was in the hospital but brought them home that afternoon. She stayed for two weeks to help care for all of us, and when she brought them to my bedside, my mom and I both burst into tears. Mareto crawled in beside me and began to cry too. It was my worst day. How could it possibly be a gift?

That night as I lay in bed scrolling through my Instagram feed, a post from Lysa TerKeurst caught my attention. She, too, was recovering from a major surgery, and I went on to read about her frightening experience and reflections:

I have a sacred realization. I have 15 staples in my belly. And I have a complete refocus on just how precious every second of every day truly is.
Might we all dare to whisper "it's a gift" to God today.
When the baby is crying and the deadlines are pressing and the stress is mounting and the enemy whispers "just get through this crappy day." Look up and shame the enemy back to hell by acknowledging today is a gift.

A gift from a good, good Father. And then look, seek, and dive deeply into what a true gift it is.[1]

Her perspective reminded me of Mareto's singsongy voice calling out from the backseat of the van, "Today is my birthday!" as we drove to the playground. Lysa nearly died from a twisted colon, and I can't imagine she had a painless recovery—yet here she was with fifteen staples in her belly writing that today is a gift.

I glanced down at my swollen belly and lifted my T-shirt to see my stitches and the incisions that would soon fade to scars. I looked at the purple-green bruises that stretched to my back, and with tears in my eyes I dared to whisper, "Today is a gift."

Then I thought back over the previous few days, and little things began to jump out at me, such as my last memory before falling asleep—of my kind and compassionate surgeon holding my hand and patting my arm and saying, "You're going to do great." How he and the anesthesiologist were proactive about my reaction to anesthesia and gave me medication to prevent post-op nausea. That alone was worth great celebration!

So I began looking for the gifts in each day—even little things that could bring me joy. Soon I was finding encouragement and hope in things as small as being able to eat a salad and not feel sick, or walk to the bathroom without needing someone to help prop me up.

A few nights later I sat on the couch in tears as my mom rubbed my back. I had just come back from the bathroom and wearily told her, "I feel terrible." As she sat next to me she listed all the things I was able to accomplish that day that I couldn't do the day before.

"You're doing great, and every day is getting a little better!" she encouraged me. I still had my hard moments, but I had people all around me to remind me that today is a gift.

The next day I was downstairs on the couch instead of upstairs in bed when Mareto came home from an outing with his dad. With wide eyes he sat next to me and pointed out, "Mommy, you're here and you have clothes. You feel better!" Seeing me in something other than a nightgown and out of bed gave him hope, and he passed that right on to me.

Looking at Mareto's encouraging smile and bright optimism reminded me anew to look at each day as a gift, as if it were my birthday.

The thing is that life brings all kinds of days, and we don't live exclusively on the mountaintop. Sometimes we must walk through the valley, and some days are just plain terrible.

Some days you go to bed in tears with a hurting heart, and other days you go to bed completely overwhelmed with joy and contentment. We can't always control what happens around us each day, but we do have control over our perspective.

WE CAN'T ALWAYS CONTROL WHAT HAPPENS AROUND US EACH DAY, BUT WE DO HAVE CONTROL OVER OUR PERSPECTIVE.

We used to sing a little song in Vacation Bible School based on Psalm 118:24: "This is the day (this is the day) / That the Lord has made (that the Lord has made) / We will rejoice (we will rejoice) / And be glad in it (and be glad in it)!" I imagine if I kept that little tune in mind, it wouldn't be so hard to treat each day like it was my birthday.

The day of my surgery was a gift, and not just because of the little things in it that I found worthy of celebration. It was a gift because God led us to that decision, and I believe I will look back at it as a pivotal moment in my life. I believe that the results of this surgery and recovery will change my life for the better. That is a gift.

Sometimes the night seems long and the pain makes it hard to see the gifts God has for us, but the sun is still there ready to break over the horizon.

Annie Downs describes this daily event in her book *Looking for Lovely*. In the chapter titled "Sunrise," she talks about watching the night become day:

> The sky starts a dark blue; the ocean looks black. The stars have retired, but the expanse is early-morning dark. The sky in front of me changes first, lightening up in blues until some pinks appear right along the horizon. The top of the sun, on the back side of the ocean, peeks over the water, and the sliver is so small and so bright it looks like a branding iron just out of the fire. It reflects off the water; and as a few minutes pass, the branding iron doubles in size. The sky responds to the fire colors in a subtle way

at first, spreading across my whole view. . . . And the sun slowly shows more and more of its morning redness, and the ocean mirrors it, and the sky mirrors it, and it seems like I can see fifty different colors, and within fifteen minutes my entire view is an explosion. It lasts for three to four minutes, and then the sun is up, the sky is blue, the clouds are white, and the day has begun.[2]

As I read this description from Annie, my mind goes to some more words that bring me hope for each new day: "The steadfast love of the LORD never ceases; his mercies never come to an end; they are new every morning; great is your faithfulness" (Lamentations 3:22–23). Each new day is a reason to give thanks.

No matter how our days end and what we're feeling when we close our eyes in the dark of the night, even if we find ourselves weeping by our beds and crying out that we simply can't do another moment, we know that the sun will rise again the next morning. There is hope and joy waiting. Because with the start of each new day, we are promised not only that the sun will rise but also that God's love and mercy will be there with it.

When we believe in what we're promised—steadfast love, never-ending mercy from heaven, and great faithfulness from the Father who created us—I wonder how it might shift our view of the day. When I keep those truths in the forefront of my mind, it really does feel like a Big-Big Playground day.

We get to begin again every morning. Life brings all

kinds of days, but we can choose how to respond to them. Will it be with joy and hope and faith and expectation? It will be for me if I'm paying attention to Mareto and following his lead as we turn left toward the Big-Big Playground.

I want to live every day with that approach. Today is a gift, a day the Lord has made and given to us. Let's treat it like it's our birthday.

Twenty-one

"Jesus Is God"

Mareto struggles with the intangible aspects of life. He loves things like letters and numbers and trains and blocks—things that remain constant, things that he can see and touch and hold in his hands. Abstract truths are a little tougher. It can be difficult for Mareto to understand that the tree is bigger than the bridge in one image but not another. Why isn't the same label applied to the tree all the time? Mareto likes things ordered and consistent . . . and tangible.

Last year I went to visit Mareto at school and to eat lunch in the cafeteria with him. I like to check on him during his day to see how he's interacting with his peers, to see if he's smiling and happy, and mostly just to get a few minutes of hugs and giggles because I miss him. When lunch ended that day, the class lined up and I took Mareto's hand. We walked through the halls back to his classroom, swinging our inter-locked hands along the way.

We were rounding the corner when Mareto tilted his head toward my face and casually mentioned, as if we'd been talking about it all day, "Jesus is God." It was a statement, not a question. He said it in the same way one might say, "Timmy's shirt is red." In a normal tone and volume—just sharing a true thing.

Mareto wasn't being forceful or making a bold decla-ration. It was a statement of faith. My breath caught in my throat as I stared down at the little boy I thought couldn't possibly understand the deity of Christ. I think I managed to say something along the lines of, "Yes, he is, sweetie." Then we hugged and kissed at the door of his classroom, and off he ran to finish his day.

I sat in the parking lot thinking about that simple but profound moment for a while. How did Mareto know that? Yes, we are a Christian family. We pray together before meals and over the children at bedtime each night. We sing songs and love others and go to church and serve together as a family. John and I share our faith with Mareto and Arsema because it's who we are and how we do life.

But faith is abstract. Even adults struggle to grasp the truths behind the practices. My children are young, and we give them information in bite-size pieces.

So I sat in that parking lot and wondered what it was that had gotten through to Mareto. Was it the time in chil-dren's church or the bedtime prayers? How did he come to understand something he couldn't see or touch or hold in his hands?

But as I sat there thinking through it, I realized how wrong it was of me to assume that Jesus and God and heaven were beyond his grasp. After all, weren't they beyond mine? How arrogant of me to assume that my son couldn't possibly grasp something like faith, but that I certainly understood the Trinity and the God who is "I am" and always has been. (Let your brain try to figure out infinity for a bit and see how it feels.)

The truth is, I don't get it. A friend of mine once described our view of God and spiritual things as looking through a knothole in a fence to see the amusement park behind it. If you have a wooden fence in your backyard, go give it a try. You might see a small picture of what lies behind that fence with your face pressed against the wood and one eye squinted shut. But what actually lies behind is a whole world that is out of your view. To say that you could draw a whole map of the park, that you know everything there is to know about it based on your peek through the hole, would be incredibly arrogant and just plain untrue.

Even if we claim to have all the answers, the truth is we don't. We actually can't wrap our minds around a God bigger than our wildest imagination, and any attempt to do so paints a thumbnail image of the real thing.

We tend to put things in a box so we can understand them better. Unknowingly, I have put Mareto in a box. I've uttered the words "He doesn't understand" more times than I can count. I've done it when we're trying to explain something at home or when we're at the playground or in a restaurant or doing a worksheet. Right in front of him I look up to John or Arsema or my parents and say, "He doesn't understand." I hate that I've done that.

Do you know why I assume Mareto doesn't understand things? Because he can't put it into words. He struggles to explain why he's upset or what he wants the toy to do or what game his friends are playing. He smiles and stares, and I assume he doesn't understand because he doesn't have the words to verbalize whatever it is that we're doing.

Last week Mareto was frustrated and crying at the kitchen table. I can't remember what the issue was, but I had one arm around him while John attempted to explain it to Mareto. He continued to cry, and I looked up to John, saying, "He just doesn't understand." For the first time ever we got a surprising response from Mareto.

"I *do* understand!" he wailed.

My heart broke, because I knew in that moment that I had underestimated my son. I had foolishly assumed that a lack of speech meant a lack of understanding. I was so very wrong. It happened a few more times that week as I caught myself saying Mareto didn't understand something. I'm working on erasing that phrase from my vocabulary.

Mareto's lack of words to describe faith, God, and heaven doesn't mean he has no understanding. After all, "How great is God—beyond our understanding!" (Job 36:26 NIV). So, why do we overcomplicate faith and claim to know things we don't? Why is it so hard for us to sit in the simplicity of faith?

The film *A Walk to Remember*, based on the novel written by Nicholas Sparks, was a big thing for us sappy romantic types when I was in college. Jamie, the main character, was dying of leukemia, and of course she and a boy named Landon fell in love. He was a bit of a mess, and she had it pretty well together. More importantly, she had faith. Jamie's faith eventually became Landon's faith, and when she died, that faith helped carry him through.

One quote from that film has stuck with me over the last fifteen years. It comes from when Landon was describing his and Jamie's love even after she had passed away: "Love is like the wind; you can't see it but you can feel it." And so it is with God.

I don't see God standing before me in the shape of a man. I don't hear his voice booming through the night, calling my name, or giving me exact directions. God, to me, is like the wind.

I don't see the wind, but I do see what the wind can do. I see the trees bend and sway. I see a runaway napkin skipping across the parking lot, away from the ice cream stand. I see the ripples made in water. I feel the wind when my hair is whipping across my face and the spring breeze rushes over my bare arms.

I don't see God, but I do see God. He's in the laughter of my children and the wonder in their eyes at Christmas. He's in the brand-new baby my friend just brought home. I see the young mother tenderly comforting her crying toddler, and an older gentleman buying flowers for his wife. I see friends laughing or crying over coffee at my kitchen table and rallying together in the best and worst moments of life. I see people in need and grieving deeply, and then I see people coming together to meet those needs and sit in the hurt. I see the sunset over the mountains and the morning mist over the river. I feel God in my heart and soul when life couldn't possibly be more beautiful and when life hurts so deeply that I don't know how to get out of bed in the morning.

Maybe Mareto knows Jesus is God because his heart can see and feel those things. Maybe Mareto knows Jesus is God because God visits and shows himself to Mareto in a special way that I don't understand. Whatever the reason, Mareto knows.

I grew up "in the church," as the saying goes. Every week we attended Sunday school and the worship service. In the summers we went to VBS. We took our first communion classes and then two years of confirmation class. I was in the youth group in high school, and we said grace before meals. Faith was stitched into the fabric of our lives during my growing-up years, and I don't remember a time not knowing God and believing he was my Creator. I don't remember a time that I didn't know Jesus loves me.

But I do remember lying in bed in the dark of night and feeling overcome with fear. And I remember gathering all my stuffed animals around me and praying for God to be with me—hoping he would appear, then sit on the edge of my bed. That never happened, of course, but he did come to me in other ways. He was in the calm that swept over my body and allowed me to fall asleep, and the stars that twinkled above me as I looked out my window. He was in the peace that settled over me after nightmares.

As the years passed and I grew older, I had more questions—but never about whether God was real. I could see him and feel him everywhere and every day, and I could see his Son too. I saw the compassion of Jesus in teachers and friends and my parents. I saw his love and service in the way our community did life together. I wondered about evil—how it could exist, and why people can be so awful—but somehow I always understood that God wins every time, even when we don't see it right away.

I had a rough first year of college. I didn't love the school I'd chosen, and I couldn't wait to transfer out. I was in a relationship that wasn't good for me, and my self-worth was taking a hit. At the close of my freshman year I ended that relationship and spent the summer a little bit lost. One evening I thought I'd reached the bottom. I didn't like myself very much, and I knew I wasn't making good choices. I sat down on my bed to make a list (because I love a good list) of all the ways I was going to fix my life. I don't remember everything on that list, but I do remember the very first bullet point.

• God

I had wandered off the path. I had stopped looking for God and seeking him in everyday moments of life and the bigger ones too. I had become reliant on myself and others to give my life meaning, and it wasn't working. I had several other bullet points, though, and I chose to focus on those first.

By the end of that summer I was still lost. Throughout the fall semester of my sophomore year I continued down a path of recklessness, making choices for myself that I knew I'd regret. By Thanksgiving break I was absolutely miserable, but you never would have known it. I'm pretty good at putting on a happy face in the midst of hard times.

Once again I sat on my bed in the little apartment I shared with three other girls. Once again I started to make a list. And once again I made that first bullet point.

- God

This time, though, I didn't keep writing. I just knew that was the answer. I didn't know how, but I knew God was going to be the only thing to help me out of the trench I'd dug for myself. I prayed for the first time in a long time. The ceiling didn't open up, and an angel didn't come chat with me in my room. But I felt a little better.

I woke up the next morning, went to class, and did whatever was next on my schedule. Then I went home and thought a lot about my faith and what it meant to me. I prayed again. Then the next day I went to class, and the next day too—and my days went on, looking similar for a while. That spring I joined a Bible study on campus and made some really special friends. I started attending a church again and felt my heart grow a little lighter each day.

Life with God is better—not easier, not devoid of pain or tragedy or missteps—but it is better. And so it has continued for me. My circumstances don't always change, and we've known hard days, but I've changed and am aware of God's presence in my life.

For me, that is the truth I can go back to when doubt creeps in. God must be real because I cannot deny his work in my life. God must be real because I see him with my heart every single day. The evidence of God is all around me.

LIFE WITH GOD IS BETTER—NOT EASIER, NOT DEVOID OF PAIN OR TRAGEDY OR MISSTEPS—BUT IT IS BETTER.

Most of us who grew up going to church can recite John 3:16 without thinking twice. It was ingrained in our minds as we sat in VBS and Sunday school, hearing: "For God so loved the world, that he gave his only Son, that whoever believes in him should not perish but have eternal life."

It's the gospel in one sentence. God loves us so crazy much that he literally sent his Son to die in our place. Anyone who believes this profoundly simple truth will live for eternity in God's kingdom. That's it. That's Christianity.

But we get caught up in the particulars, don't we? We want to know the rules and the ways. We want to know who, what, where, and when . . . also the how and why. We aren't content with the simple truth of God's love, sacrifice, and redemption.

A couple thousand years ago, people struggled with this concept too. A man asked Jesus what the most important commandment was. He wanted to know what rules to follow, how to live, so that he could go to heaven. He was sincere, and Jesus answered: "You shall love the Lord your God with all your heart and with all your soul and with all your mind. This is the great and first commandment. And a second is like it: You shall love your neighbor as yourself. On these two commandments depend all the Law and the Prophets" (Matthew 22:37–40).

It's simple: Love God and love others. Everything hinges on these two things. You can sum up all Ten Commandments and every prophecy in those words. Love God. Loving God means believing in him. Love others. Loving others is done imperfectly at best, but we do it because God is love.

We don't need a fancy degree to have meaningful faith that brings peace and joy. It doesn't take a seminary education to understand the gospel and have faith in God. It's okay to not understand all the ins and outs of the Creator of the universe. You don't need to know the meaning of the word *eschatology* to see God.

We don't have to understand everything to believe in something bigger than ourselves. In fact, that itself is the faith part—we haven't seen Jesus literally, but we see him with our hearts and souls. We might not have all the right words, but we have assurance. Mareto believes because he has faith, and it's just that simple. Jesus is God.

Conclusion

WIDE OPEN

These pages are as much a life manual for me today as they were when I first put pen to paper (or finger to keyboard). I often forget to take my own advice, and I struggle to find my peace, my courage, and my faith. I get tired and discouraged. I look down at the little people I'm supposed to be teaching and realize somewhere along the way I stopped listening.

The thing is, I am still learning—and I don't think that will ever stop. I'm not a brand-new mom anymore, but I'm not yet a seasoned mother. Mareto is just starting elementary school, and the lessons he will teach me in the next five, ten, and fifteen years will be very different from the ones he teaches me today. But the truths he illuminates for me now are no less valuable than the things I will learn from him later. I don't want to forget.

Every step of the journey is important.

I'm so grateful for the words I find in Zechariah 4:10: "Do not despise these small beginnings, for the LORD rejoices to see the work begin" (NLT).

The beginning of a story is just as important as the middle and the end. Our children can be our greatest teachers if we let them. Our struggles can light a path we never would have looked for, and we can find truth, freedom, and joy in the most unexpected places.

Where is your story today? Are you at the start of something, brimming over with excitement and anticipation? Are you stuck in the middle and fumbling around for the light switch? Are you facing a trial you never saw coming and find yourself paralyzed with fear and denial? Are you exhausted by life? Afraid? Uncertain? Are you looking for hope and joy and love and wondering where it all went?

Start back at the beginning. Throw out your old, preconceived ideas about what a successful life should look like, and restart with a new perspective. Grieve your losses and look for a new path as you accept the things you never expected or wanted. Take a break—go for a hike, take a swim, sit out on the porch and listen to the rhythm of the crickets singing. Call a sitter and take an afternoon nap. Breathe deeply. Cry when you need to.

Open your doors and your heart. Make a new friend, or two, or ten. Love bigger than you thought you could, and find that expanding your borders increases your capacity to love and receive love.

Rest in the knowledge that you are already enough.

Today. Right now. You are valuable, worthy, and important. Show up for life even when you don't feel ready. There will be days of small joys and big joys and everything in between. It all matters, and it's all important.

And, most of all, live moment to moment with your heart wide open, knowing that whatever comes ... it's okay about it.

Acknowledgments

This wasn't the book I thought I'd write first. This was the book I thought I'd write later on, maybe after my kids were grown and I felt like I was "ready." But it turns out it *was* the book I was supposed to write first, and it wouldn't have been possible without the support of so many others. The few words I share in this section aren't enough to express the ocean of gratitude I have for each person who has touched my life and this story.

John, thank you for loving me and choosing each day to do life with me. You have always been my biggest cheerleader—encouraging me out of my comfort zone but always right there holding my hand. You see me as the person I hope to grow into someday. I'm so glad we picked each other. LOVE.

Mareto, you inspire me. I look at you and know that with God all things are possible. You've brought me hope and peace, and the world is brighter because of you. You are my favorite boy in the whole wide world, and I love you.

Arsema, you delight me. I never thought one person could possess so much sparkle until I met you. You have such a contagious zest for life, and you bring me so much joy. You are my best girl in the whole wide world, and I love you.

Dad and Mom, thank you for believing in me from day one. Thank you for a childhood of adventure and once-in-a-lifetime experiences. I'll never stop trying to make you proud. I love you both.

Amber and Kevin, I might not have acted like it when we were younger, but I am so grateful to be sandwiched in the middle of you two. You each amaze me, and I love you.

My girlfriends near and far, I can't possibly list you all out by name, but you know who you are. From texts to phone calls to emails to coffee dates and nights out, you've helped me keep my sanity. You make life richer, and I love each one of you dearly.

Lisa, you took a chance on me, and I can't thank you enough. After our first phone call I not only knew you would be the perfect agent for me, but I also felt like we would be good friends. Thank you so much for taking me under your wing, believing in me, and championing my ideas.

Jessica, I felt connected to you from our first conference call and knew my book would be safe in your hands. You saw straight to the heart of my message and worked by my side to shape and mold that message into this book. Thank you from the bottom of my heart.

My Thomas Nelson team, this experience has shown me just how much work and detail goes into publishing a book.

I am amazed by all the pieces that come together to create a finished product, and I am eternally grateful. Thank you for allowing me to be a part of this family; it is truly an honor.

My readers, none of this would be possible without you. Thank you for reading the words I release through my blog and various outlets and now this book. Thank you for seeing your own stories in mine. We belong to each other.

Notes

Chapter 2: "Christmas Is Ruined!"

1. Glennon Doyle Melton, "2011 Lesson #2: Don't Carpe Diem," *Momastery*, January 4, 2012, http://momastery.com/blog /2012/01/04/2011-lesson-2-dont-carpe-diem.

Chapter 3: "You're Making Me Feelings"

1. Temple Grandin, *The Autistic Brain: Thinking Across the Spectrum* (Boston: Houghton Mifflin Harcourt, 2013), 194.

Chapter 5: "My Batteries Is All Gone!"

1. Paul Vitello, "Taking a Break from the Lord's Work," *New York Times*, August 1, 2010, www.nytimes.com/2010/08/02 /nyregion/02burnout.html.

Chapter 9: "Look! The Tree Rainbow!"

1. Mary Beth Chapman, *Choosing to See* (Grand Rapids: Revell, 2010), 224.

Chapter 11: "Stephen's in Danger!"

1. Fred Rogers, *The World According to Mr. Rogers* (New York: Hyperion, 2003), 187.

Chapter 12: "It's Too Loud My Ears!"

1. "How a week of camping resets the body clock," *The Conversation*, August 1, 2013, http://theconversation.com/how-a-week-of-camping-resets-the-body-clock-16557.

Chapter 14: "I Can. I Will. I Believe."

1. C. S. Lewis, *The Lion, the Witch and the Wardrobe* (New York: HarperCollins, 2000), 80.
2. To be clear, I use Mareto's phrase "I can. I will. I believe." to help me through hard things: moments of fear and anxiety. I do not want to suggest that I believe it should be used in place of medical and/or therapeutic intervention for those who need it. Nor am I suggesting that one can simply talk themselves out of anxiety/panic disorders. Mareto's phrase is a tool and a helpful reminder for me in tough moments. Please seek professional help if you are struggling with panic and/or anxiety.

Chapter 15: "Or Yes, or No?"

1. Barry Schwartz, *The Paradox of Choice: Why More Is Less* (New York: Harper Perennial, 2004), 25.
2. Ellen DeGeneres, *Here and Now*, www.amazon.com/Ellen-DeGeneres-Here-Now/dp/B007Q3527K/ref=sr_1_1?s=instant-video&ie=UTF8&qid=1473185308&sr=1-1&keywords=ellen+degeneres.
3. Schwartz, *The Paradox of Choice*, 78.

Chapter 18: "Cheese and Crackers!"

1. Elizabeth Gilbert, *Big Magic: Creative Living Beyond Fear* (New York: Riverhead, 2015), 93.
2. Myquillyn Smith, *The Nesting Place* (Grand Rapids: Zondervan, 2014), 164.

Chapter 19: "It's a Job-a-doo!"

1. Dana Schuster, "Ivana Trump on how she advises Donald— and those hands," *New York Post*, April 3, 2016, http://nypost .com/2016/04/03/ivana-trump-opens-up-about-how-she -advises-donald-his-hands.

Chapter 20: "Today Is My Birthday!"

1. Lysaterkeurst. Instagram post. June 20, 2016. https://www .instagram.com/p/BG4BORVwC49.
2. Annie F. Downs, *Looking for Lovely: Collecting the Moments That Matter* (Nashville: B&H, 2016), 58–59.

About the Author

LAUREN CASPER is the founder of the popular blog LaurenCasper.com, where she shares her thoughts on life, parenting, and faith. She is a top contributor to the TODAY Parenting Team, and has had numerous articles syndicated by the *Huffington Post*, the *TODAY* show, Yahoo! News, and several other publications. She also has the joy of serving on the Created for Care team, a nonprofit ministry dedicated to serving foster and adoptive families. Lauren speaks in various locations around the country at conferences, retreats, and church events.

Lauren has been happily married to her husband, John, since 2005. Together they have two children—Mareto and Arsema—who came home from Ethiopia in 2011 and 2012. The Caspers make their home in the Shenandoah Valley of Virginia.